COLOR THE WORLD

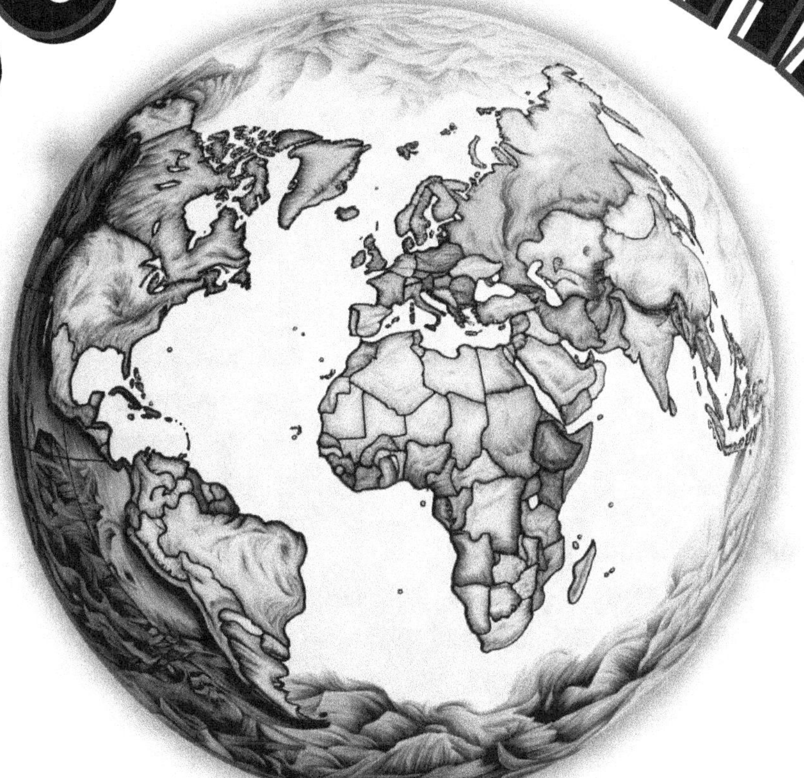

An Adult Coloring Book Featuring The Most Iconic Places & Faces On Earth!

Diana Ng

Copyright 2024. All Rights Reserved. Produced using midjourney.com

Love this coloring book? Share your review on Amazon to help others find & experience *Color The World*!

It's easy! Simply scan this QR code to leave your honest review!

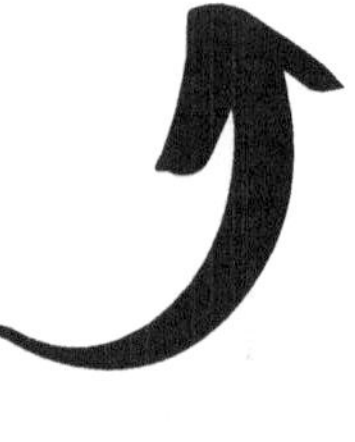

Thank you so much! I appreciate it!

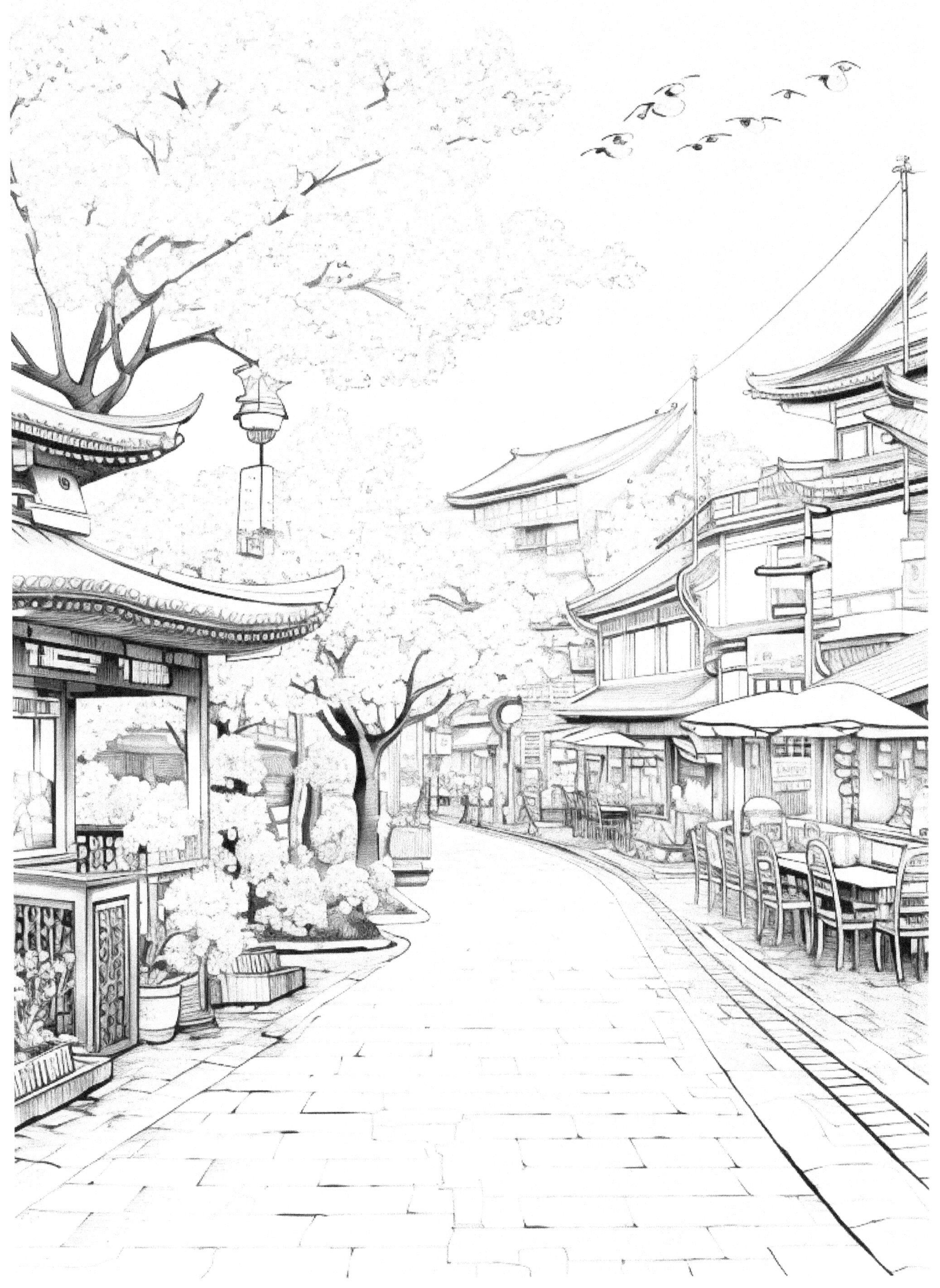

Kyoto, Japan

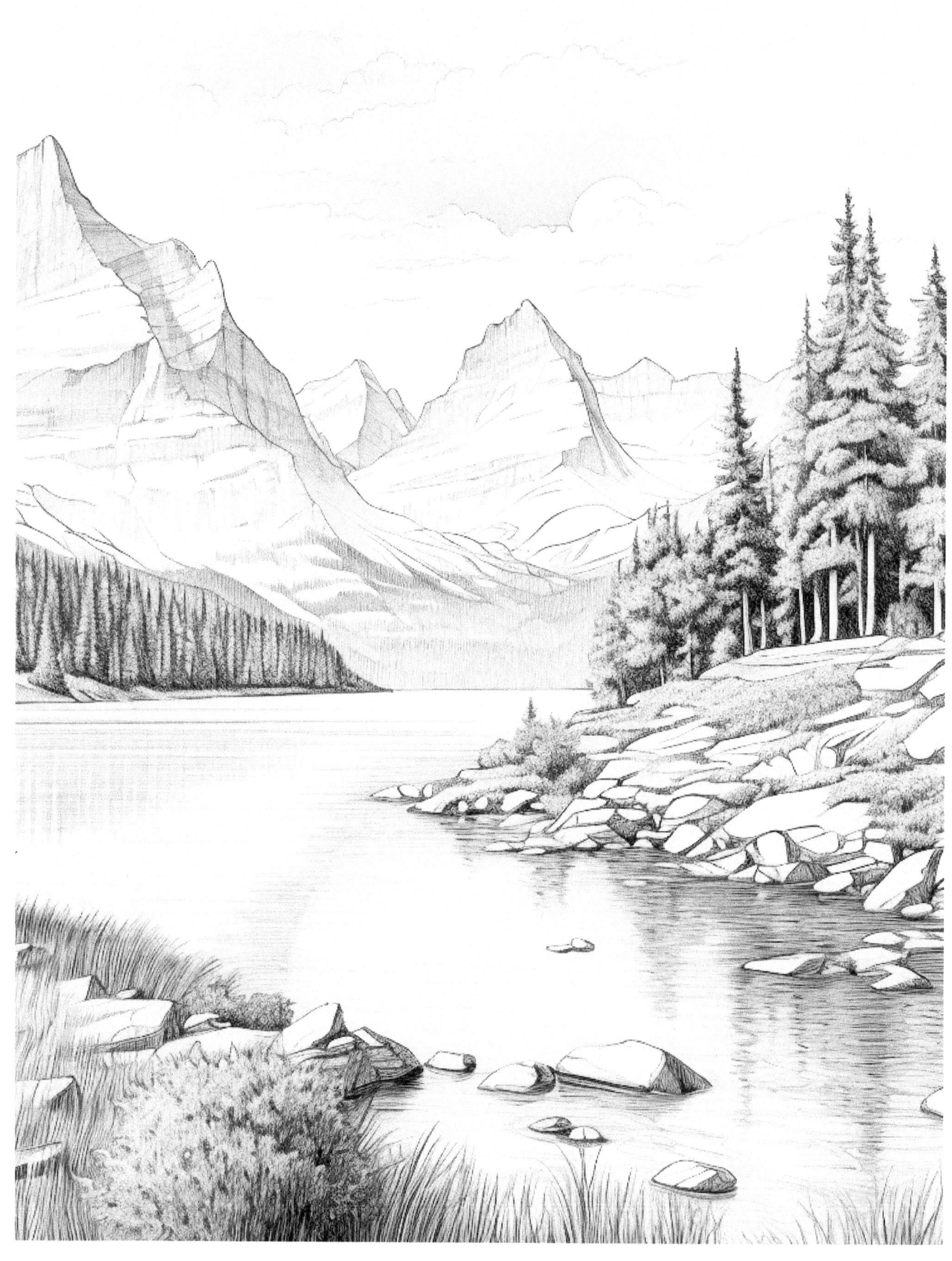

Glacier National Park, USA

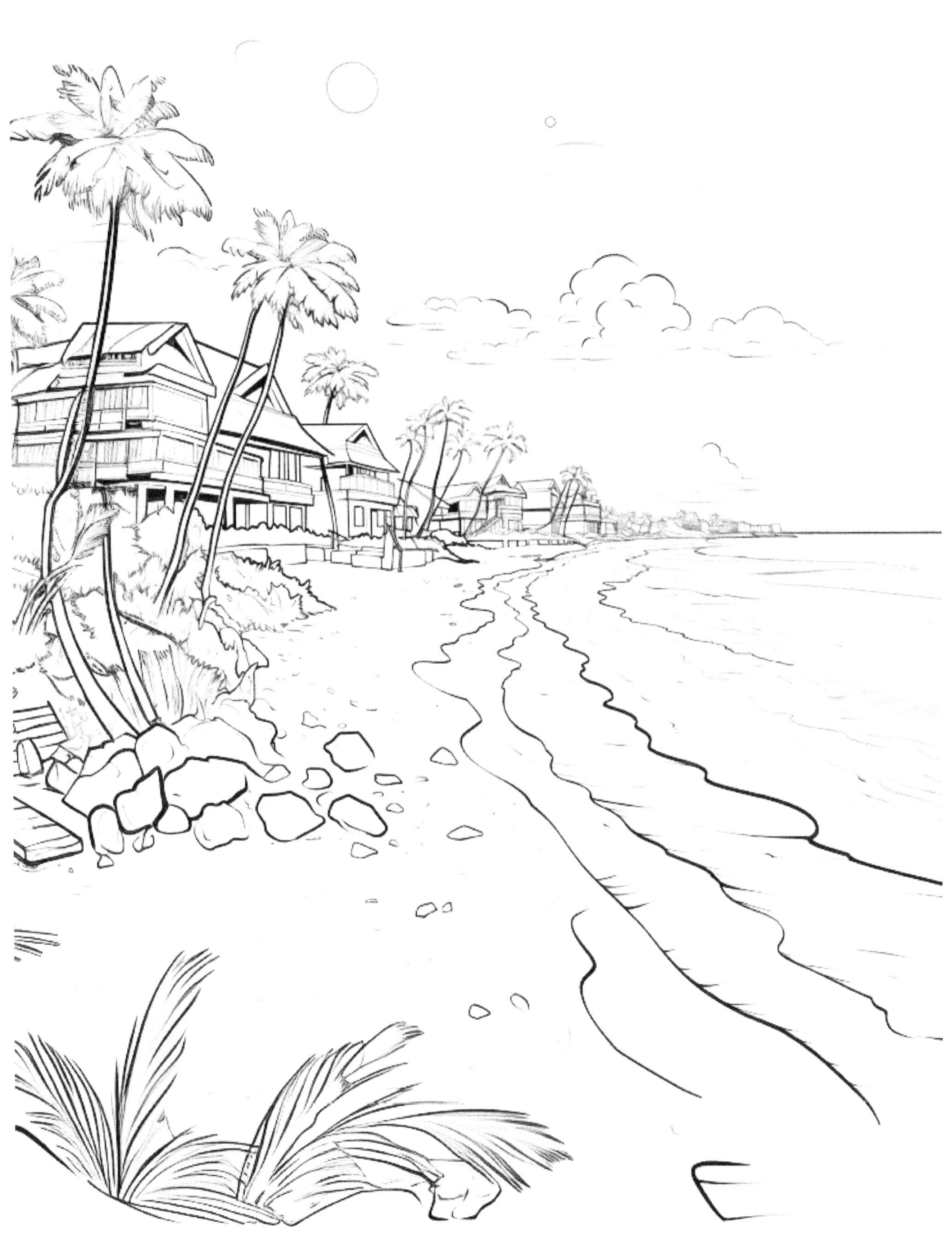
Bali, Indonesia

Auckland, New Zealand

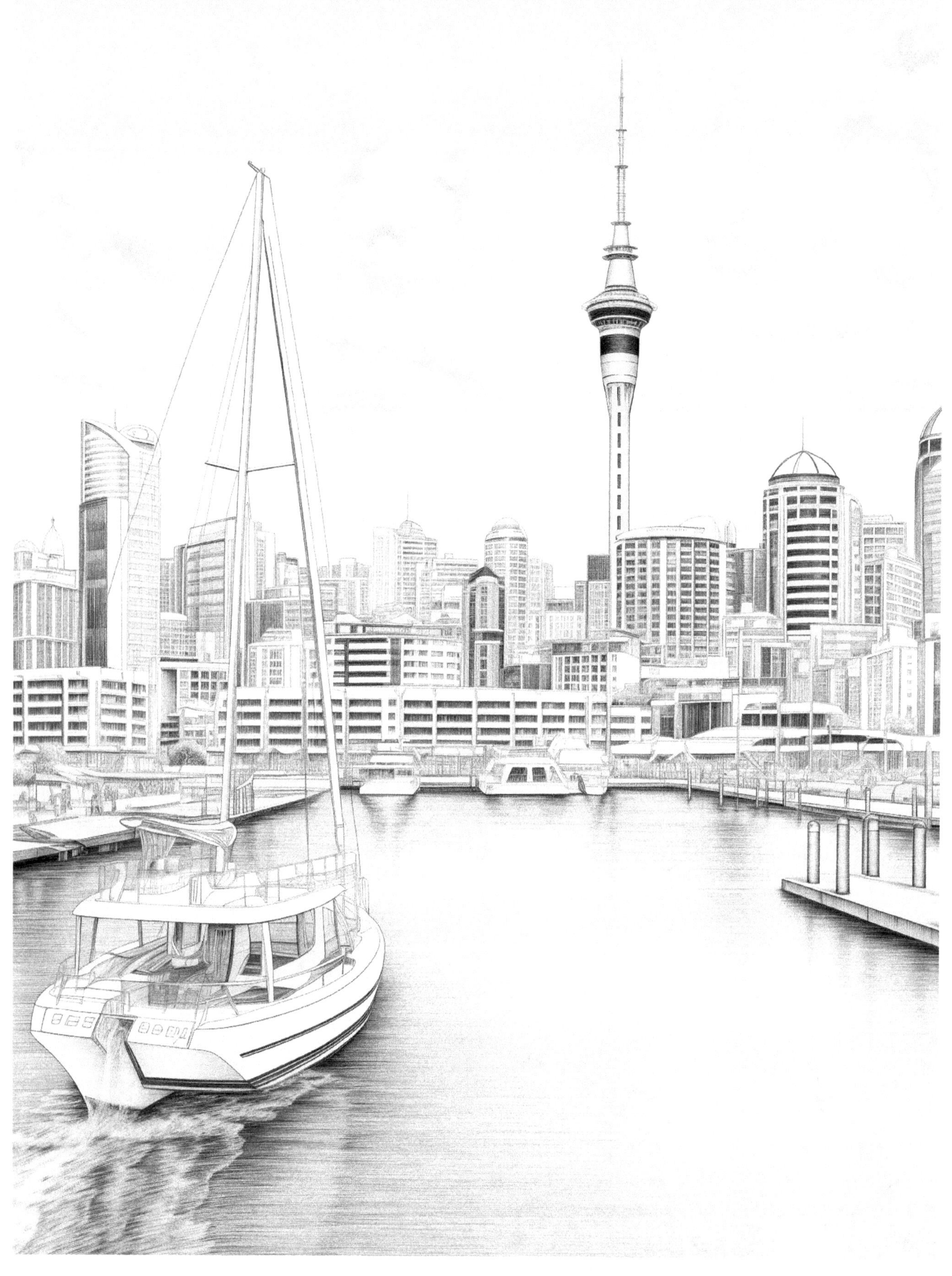

Buckingham Palace, UK

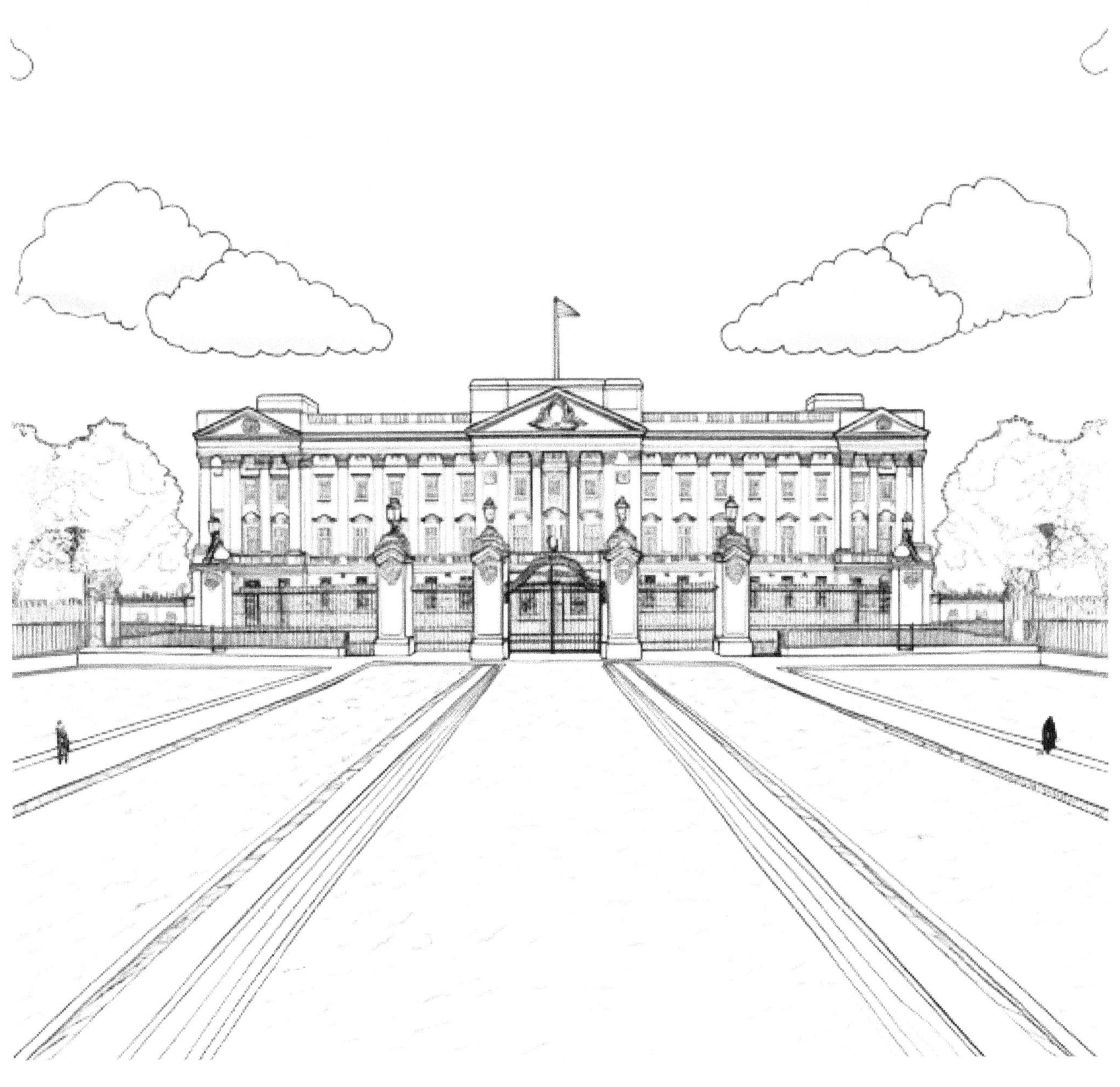

Venice, Italy

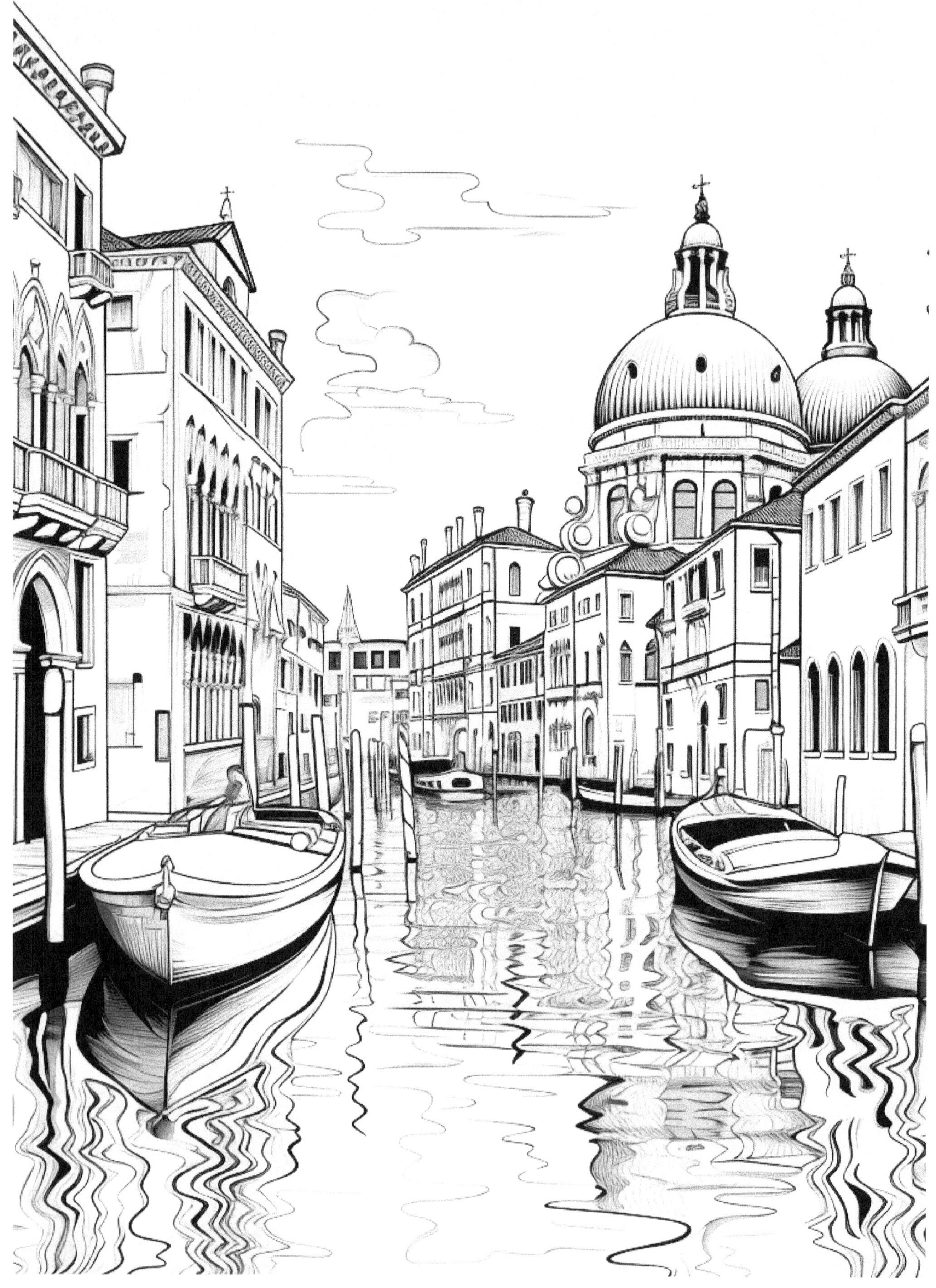

Korean Couple

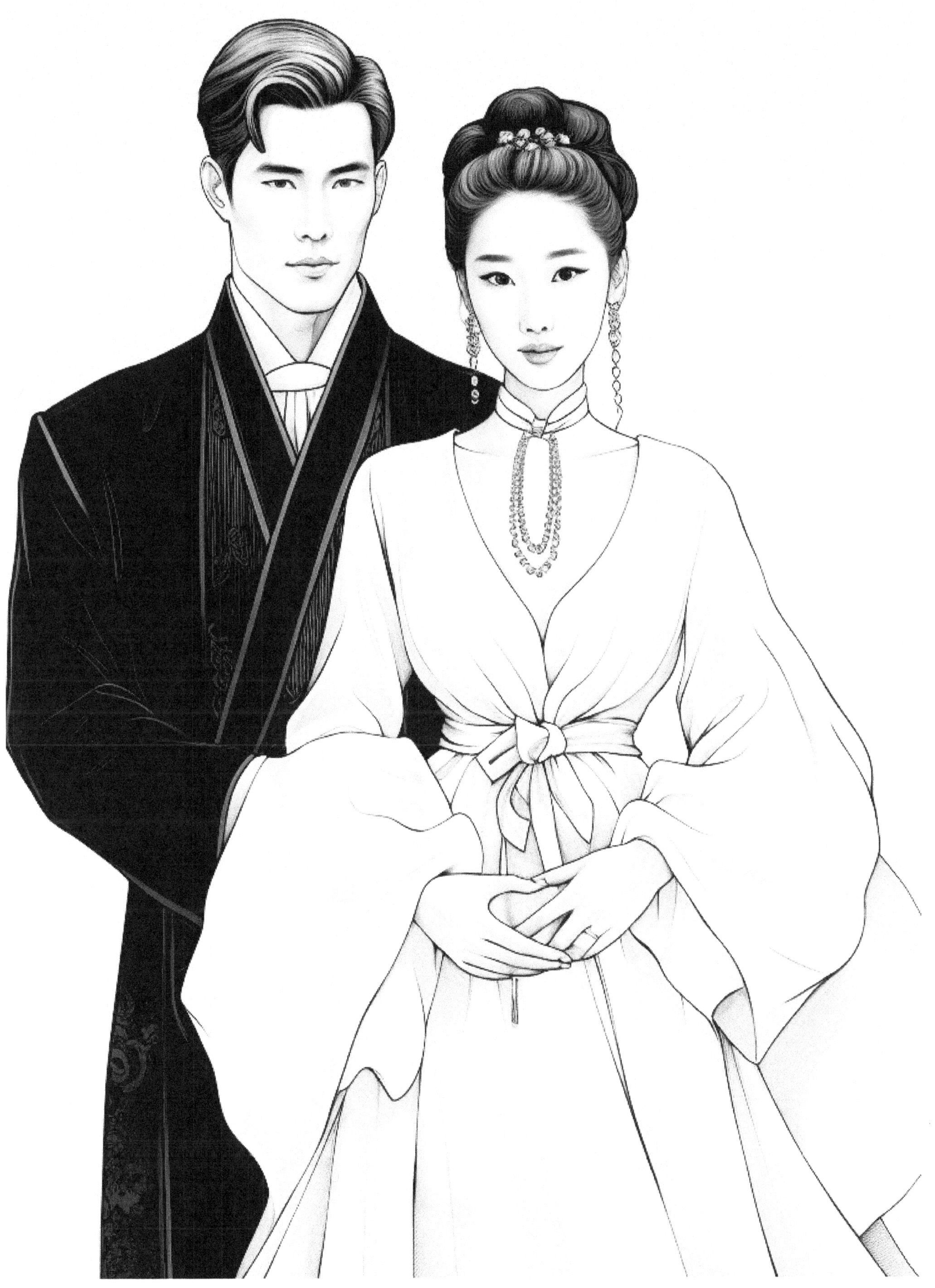

Mount Everest

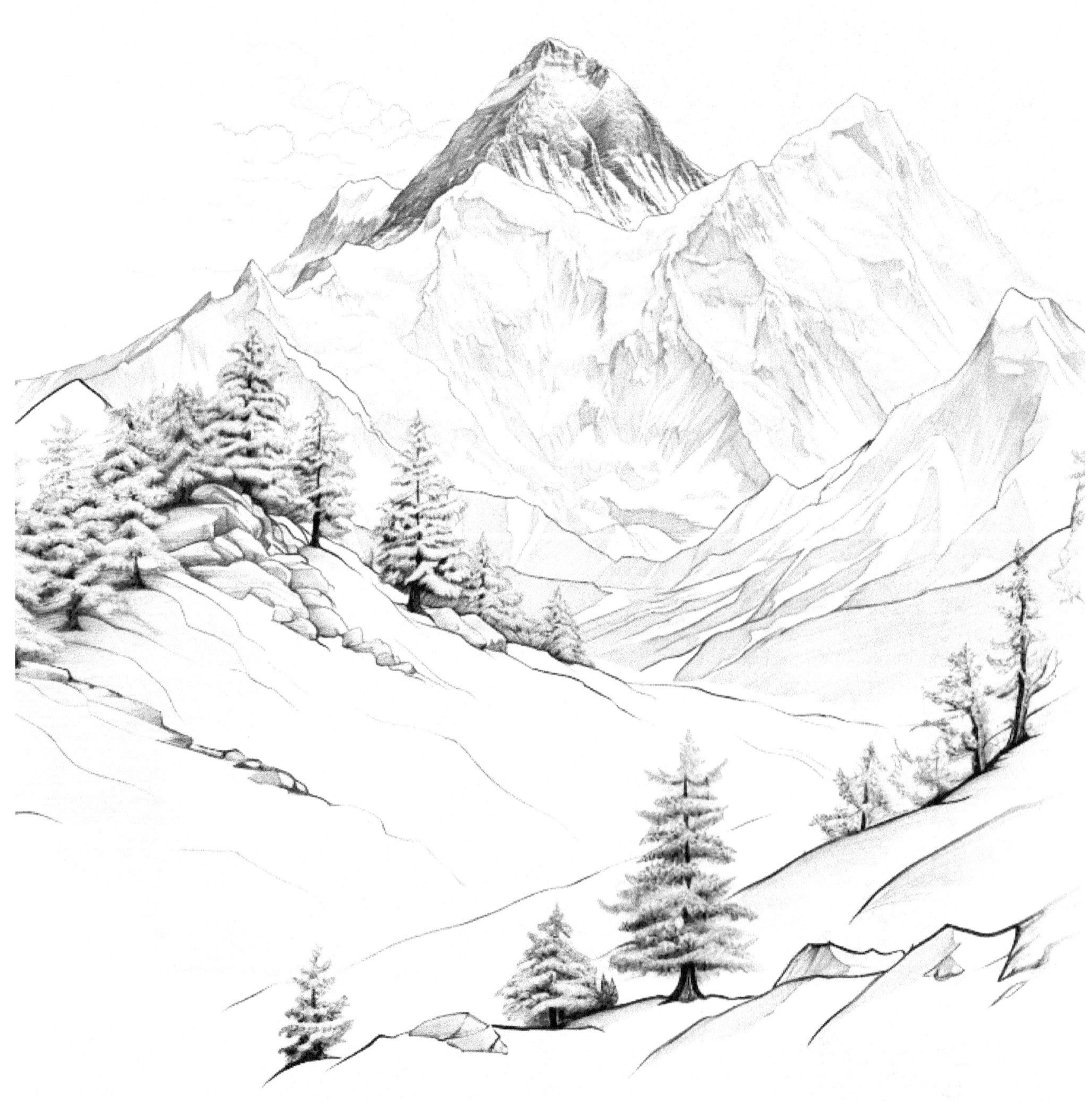

Waikiki Beach, Hawaii

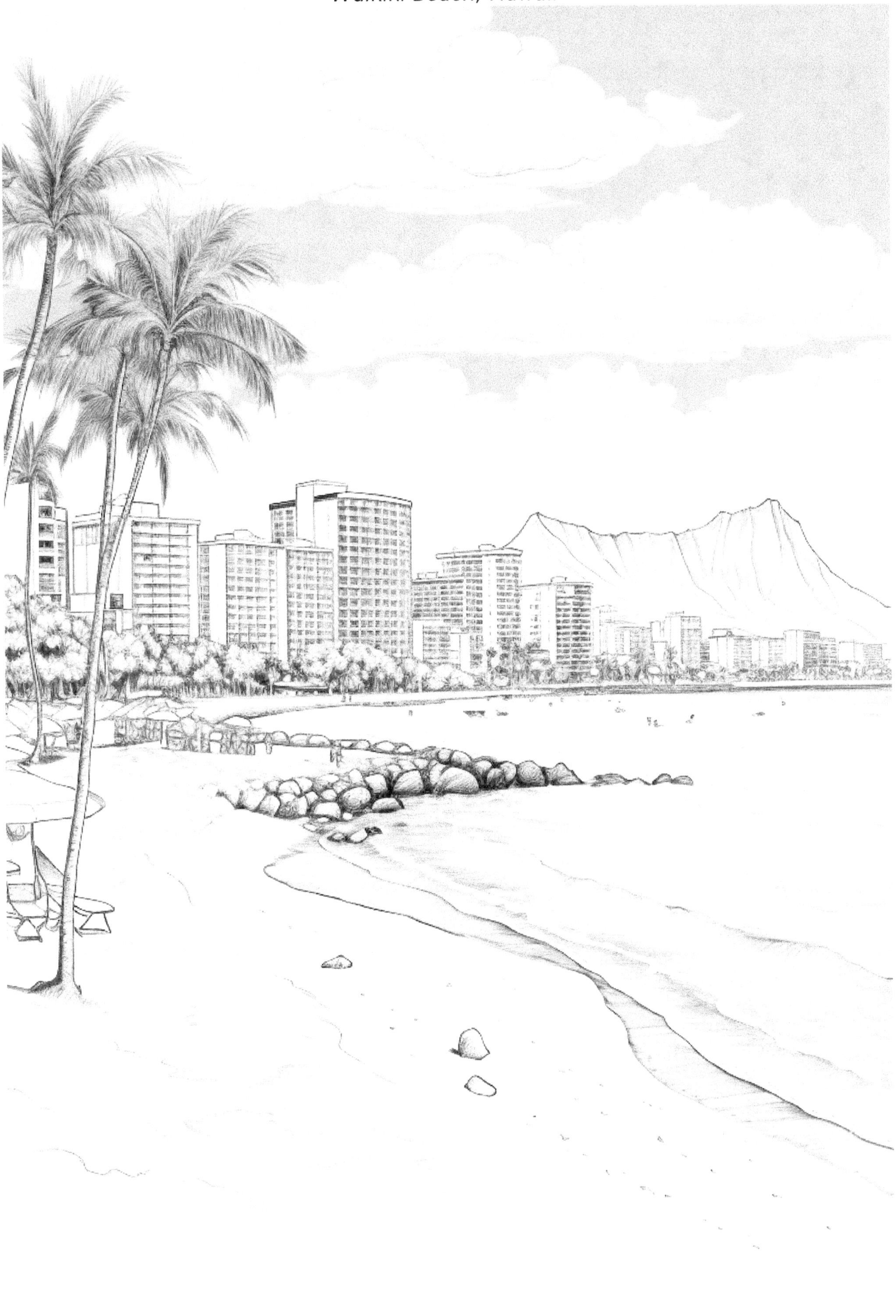

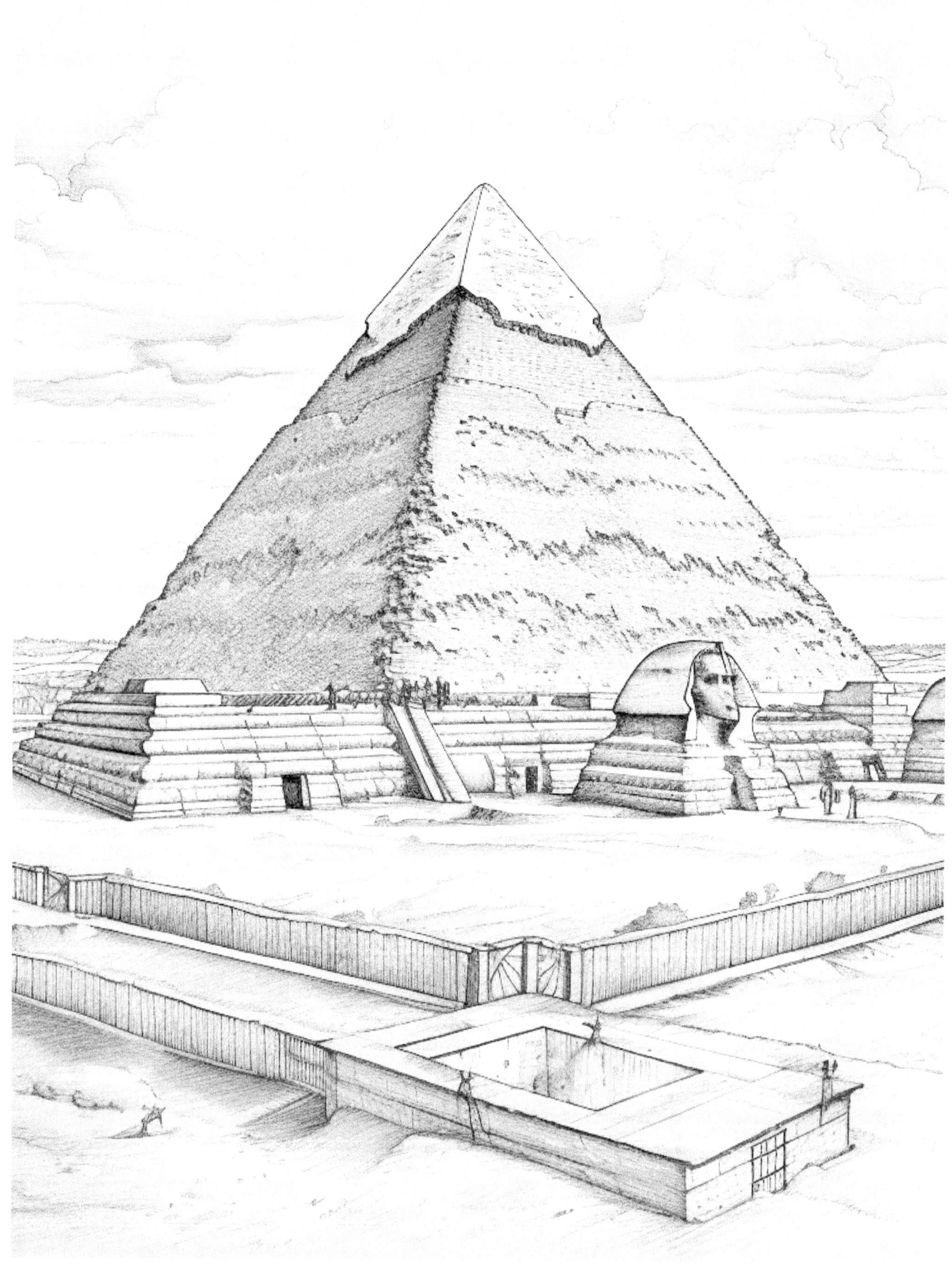

Pyramid of Giza, Egypt

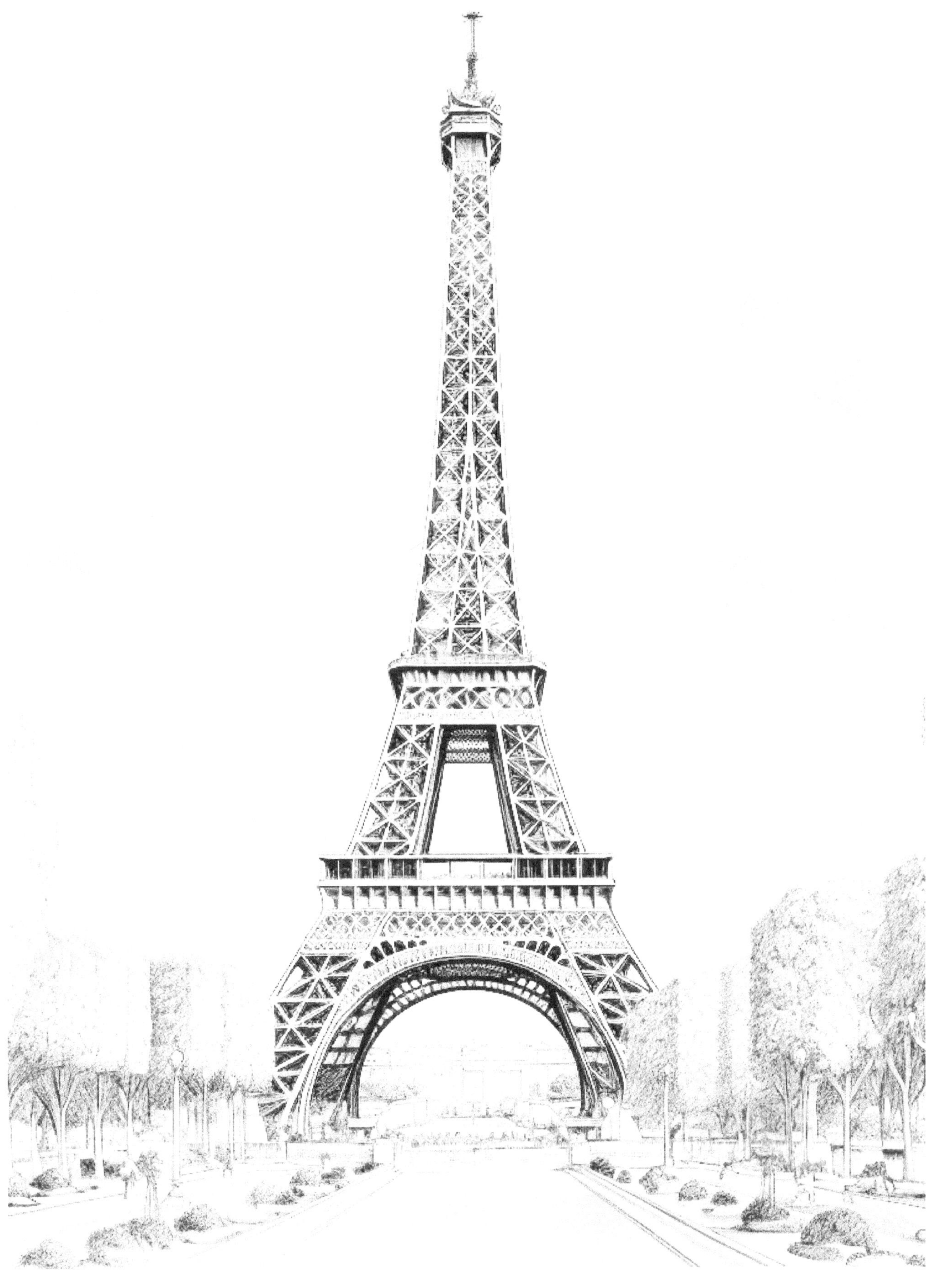

Eiffel Tower, Paris

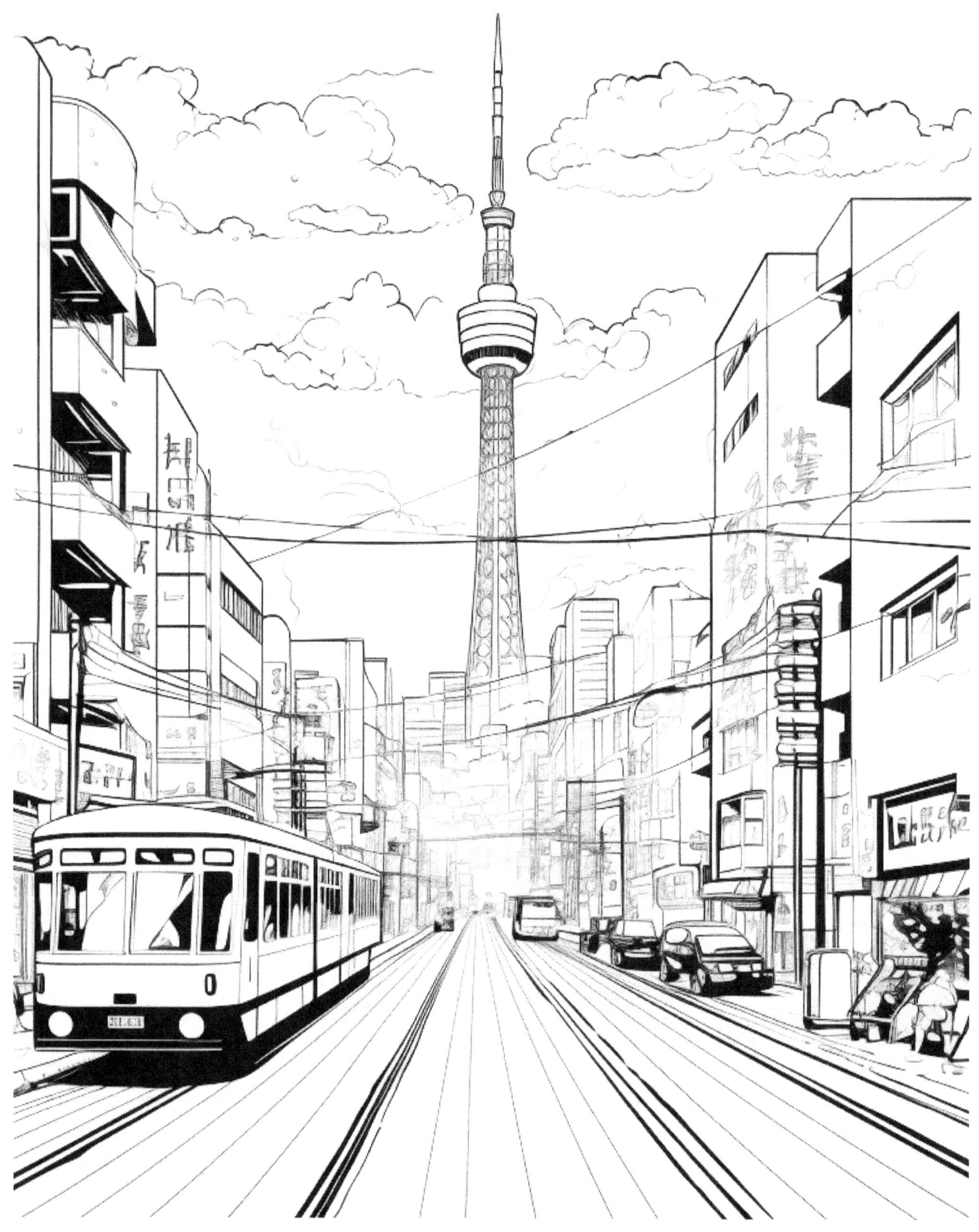

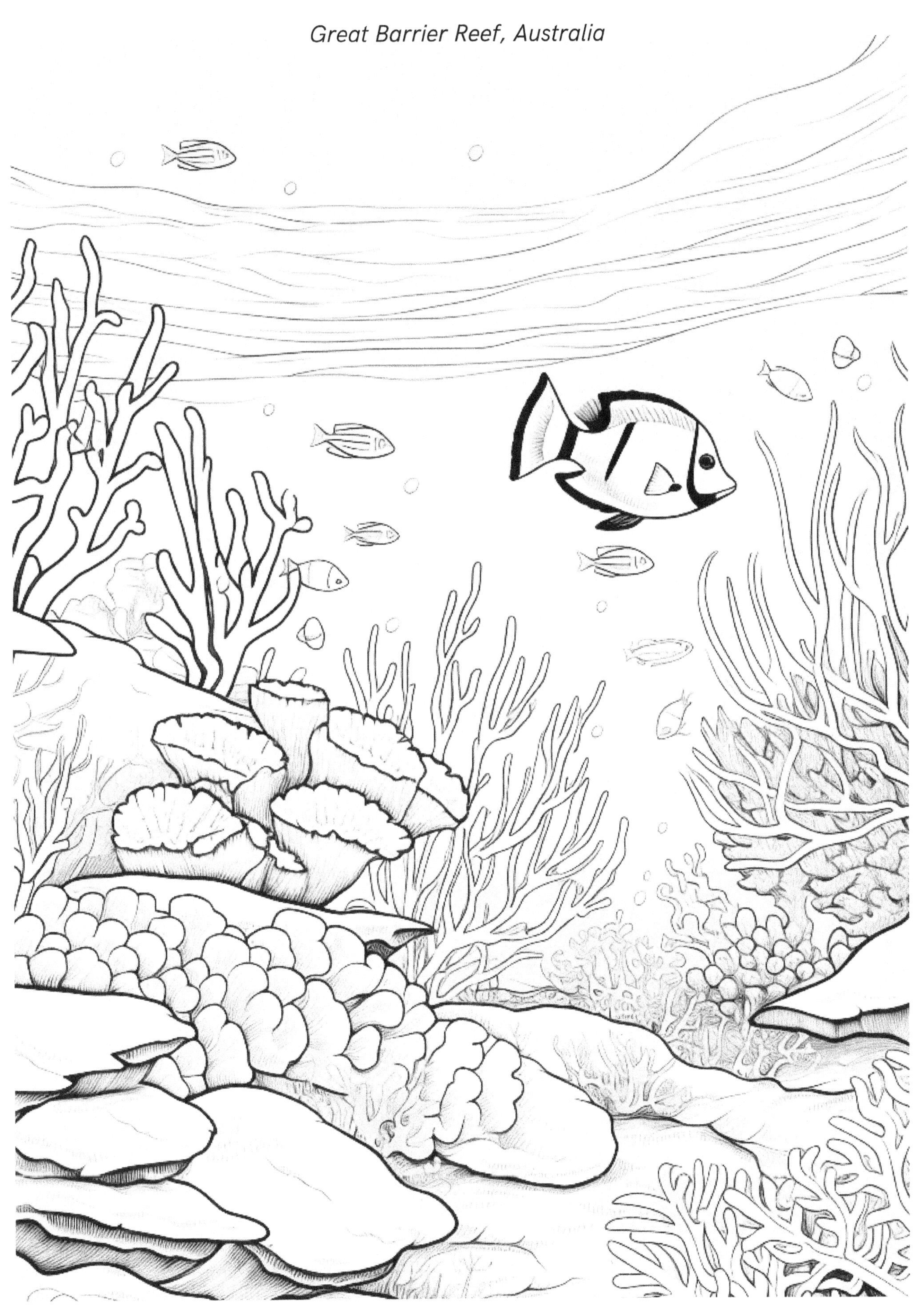

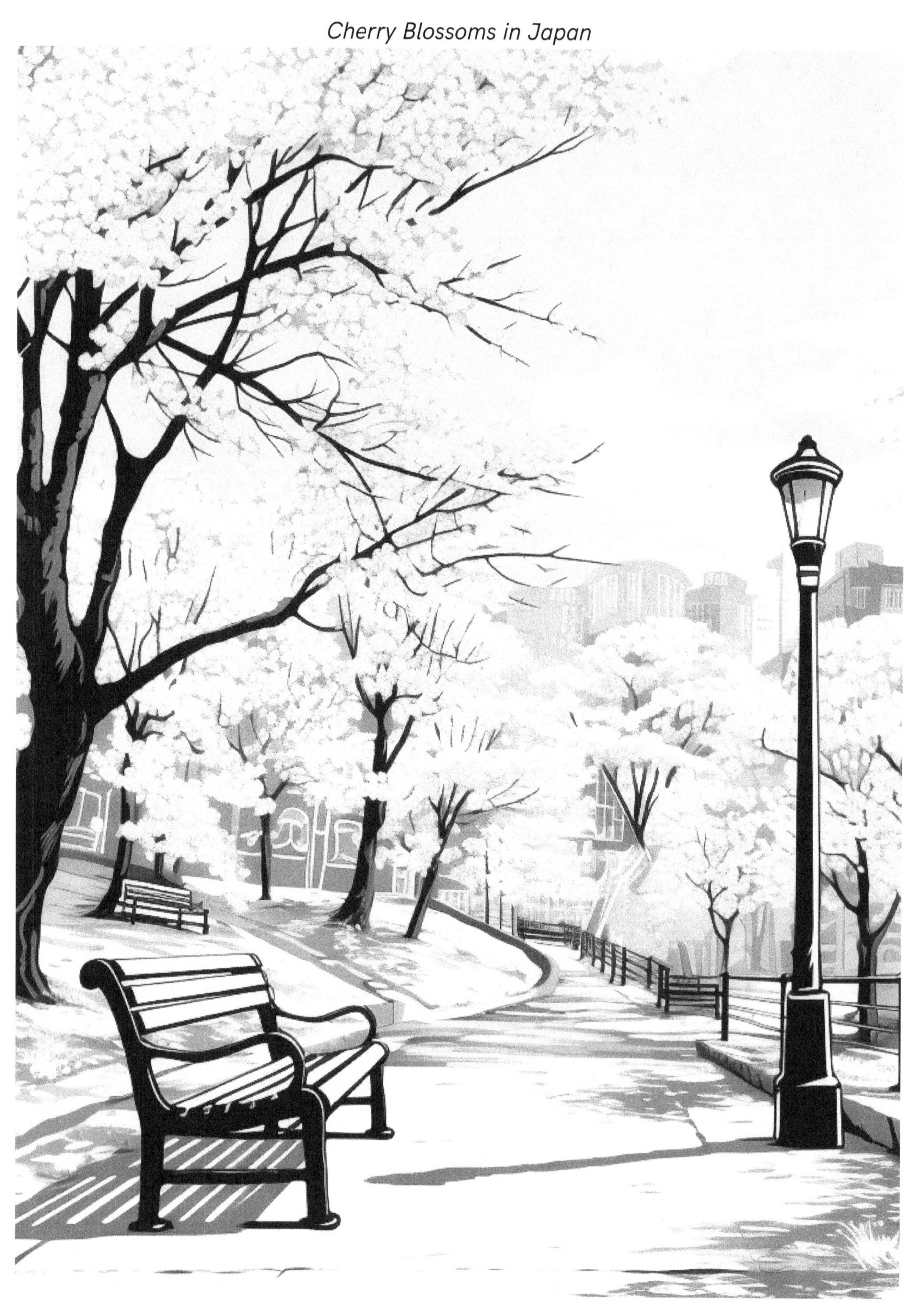

Cherry Blossoms in Japan

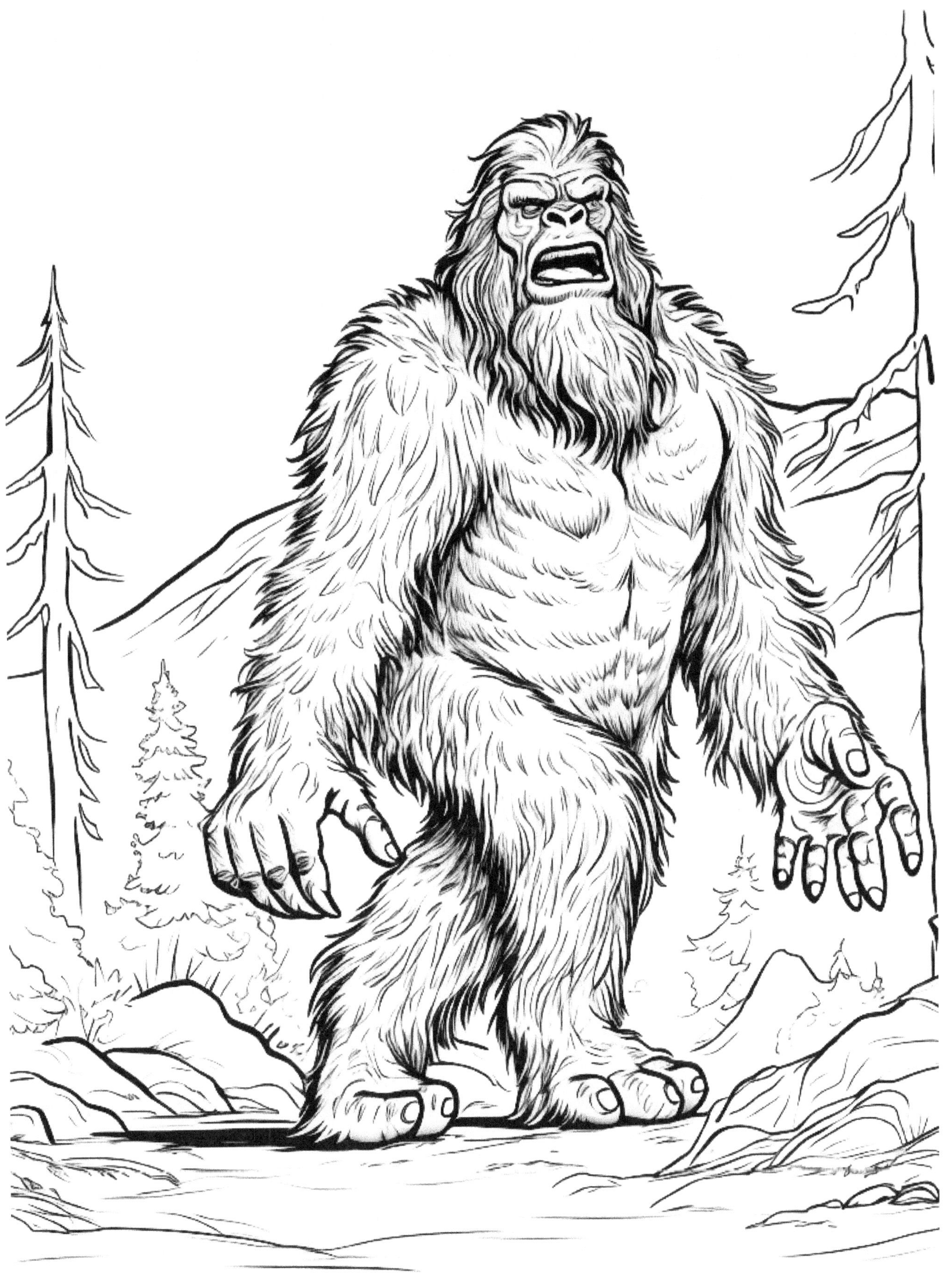

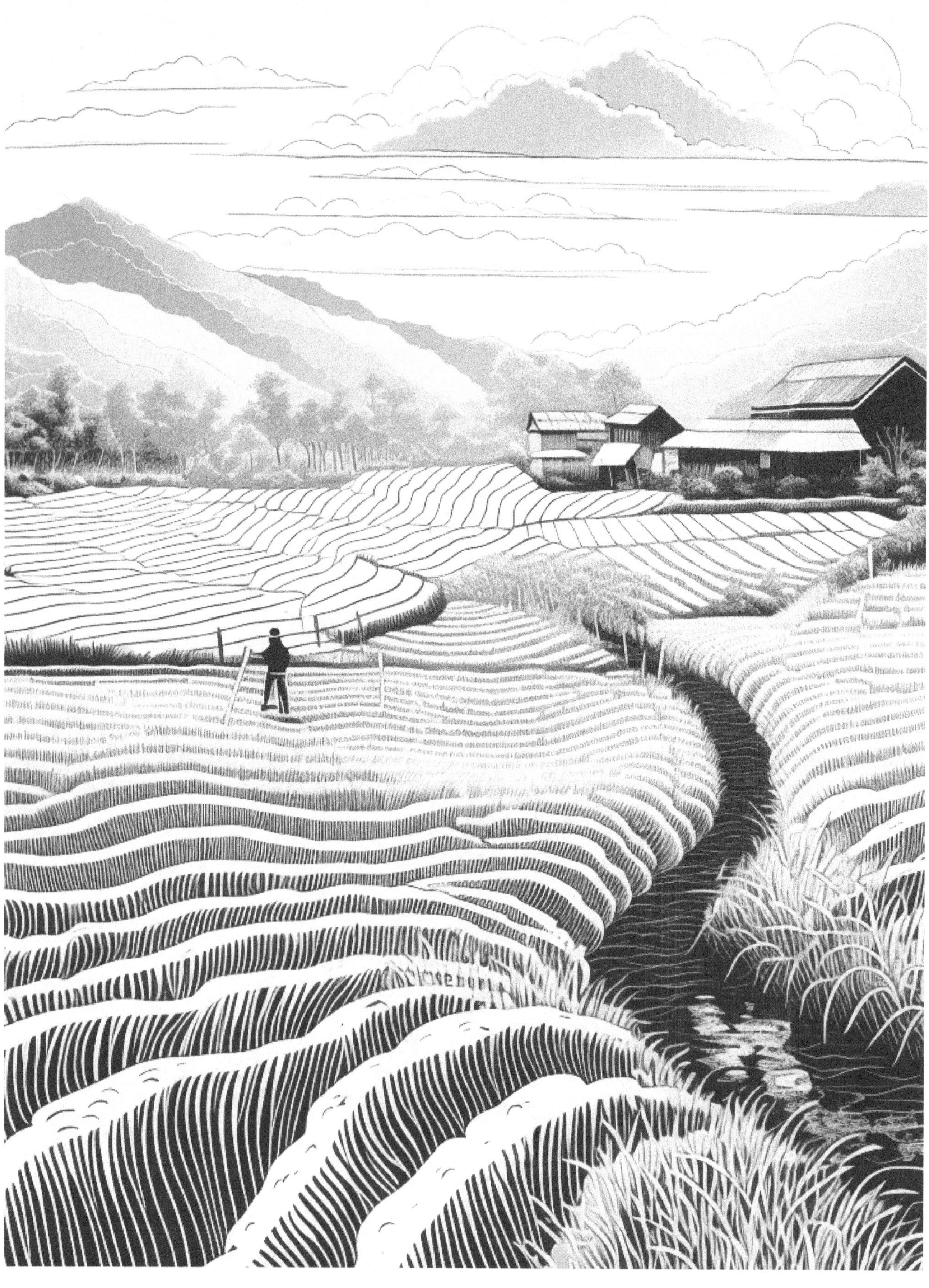

Vietnam

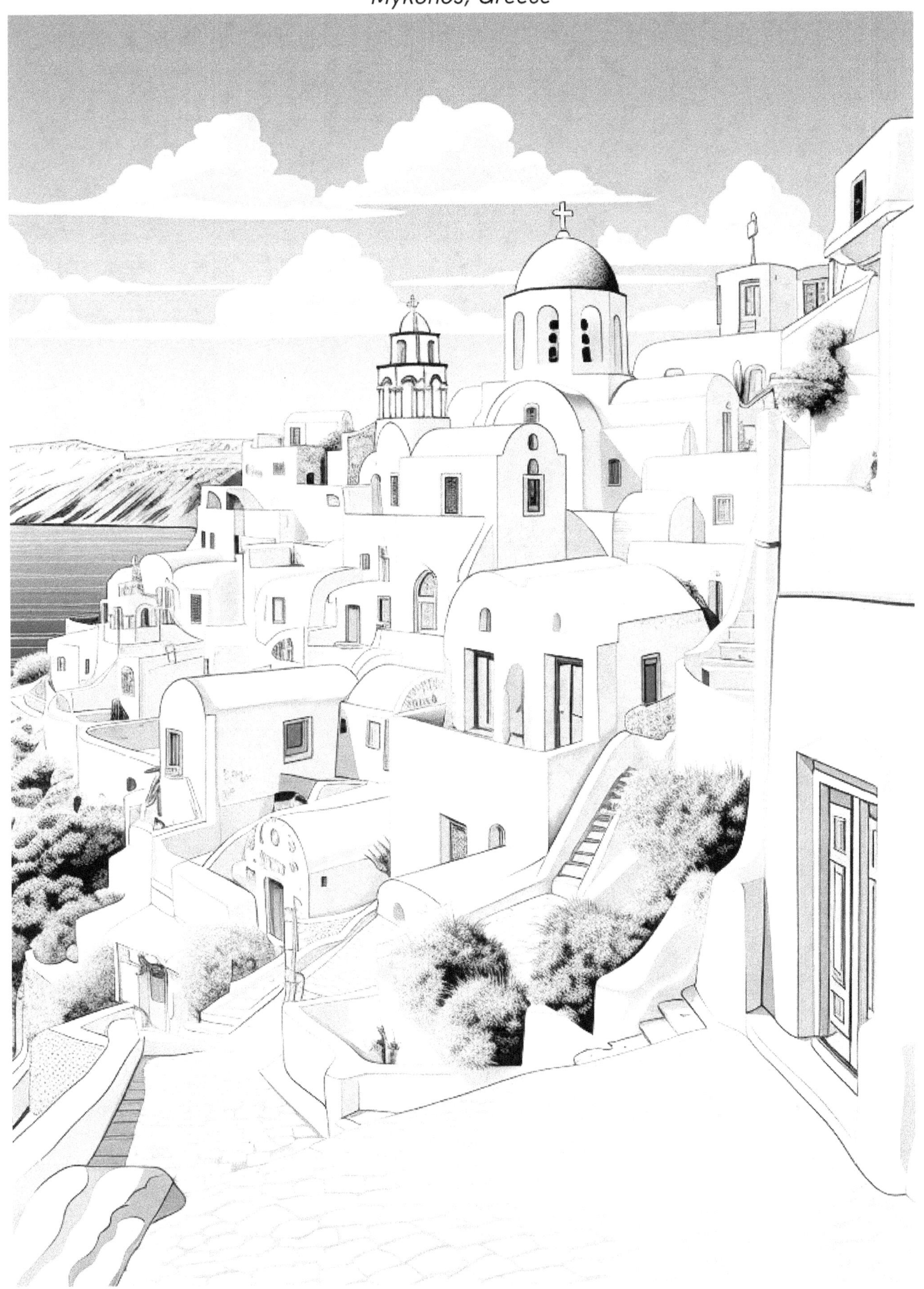

Great Wall of China

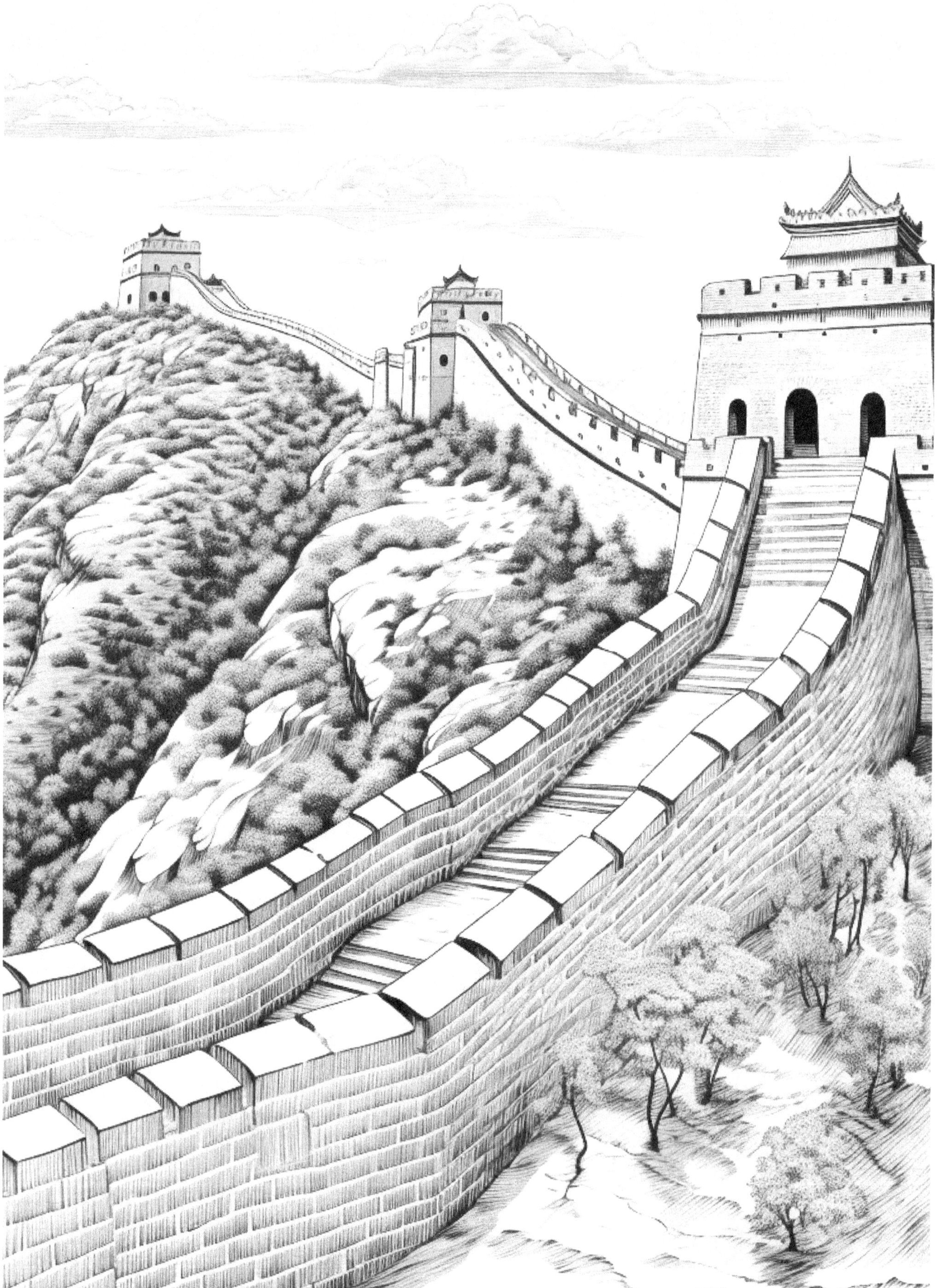

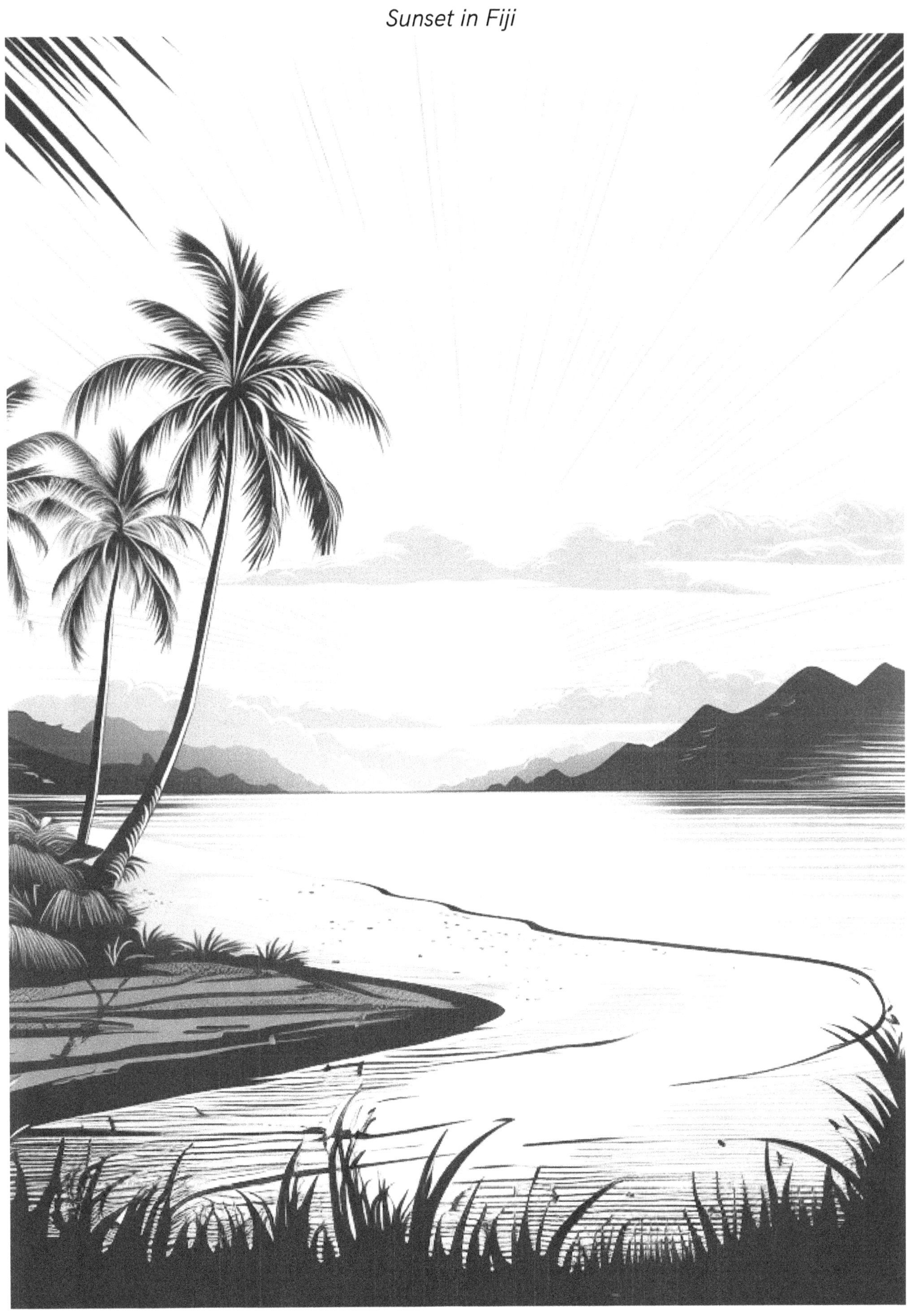

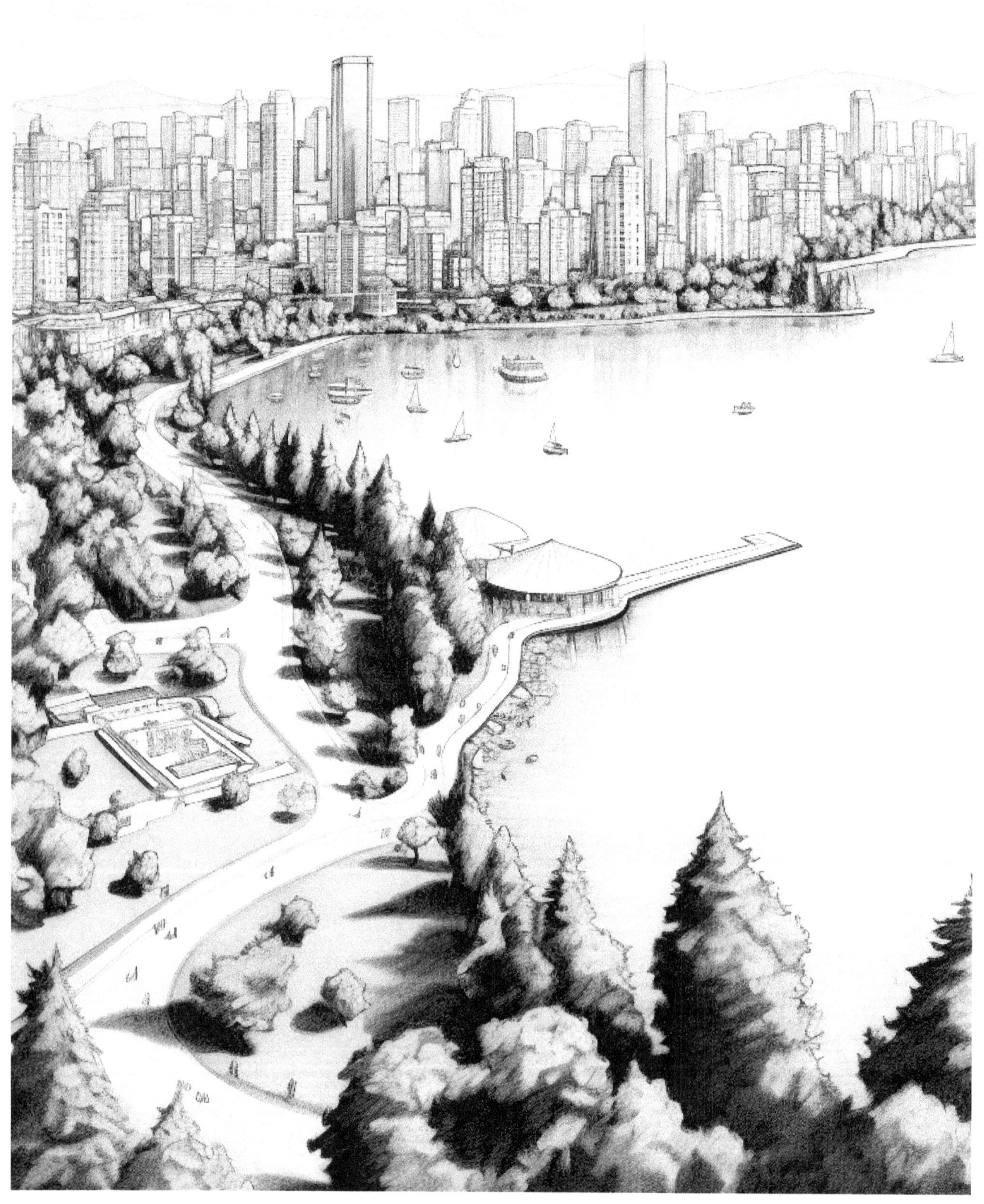

Vancouver, Canada

Times Square, NYC

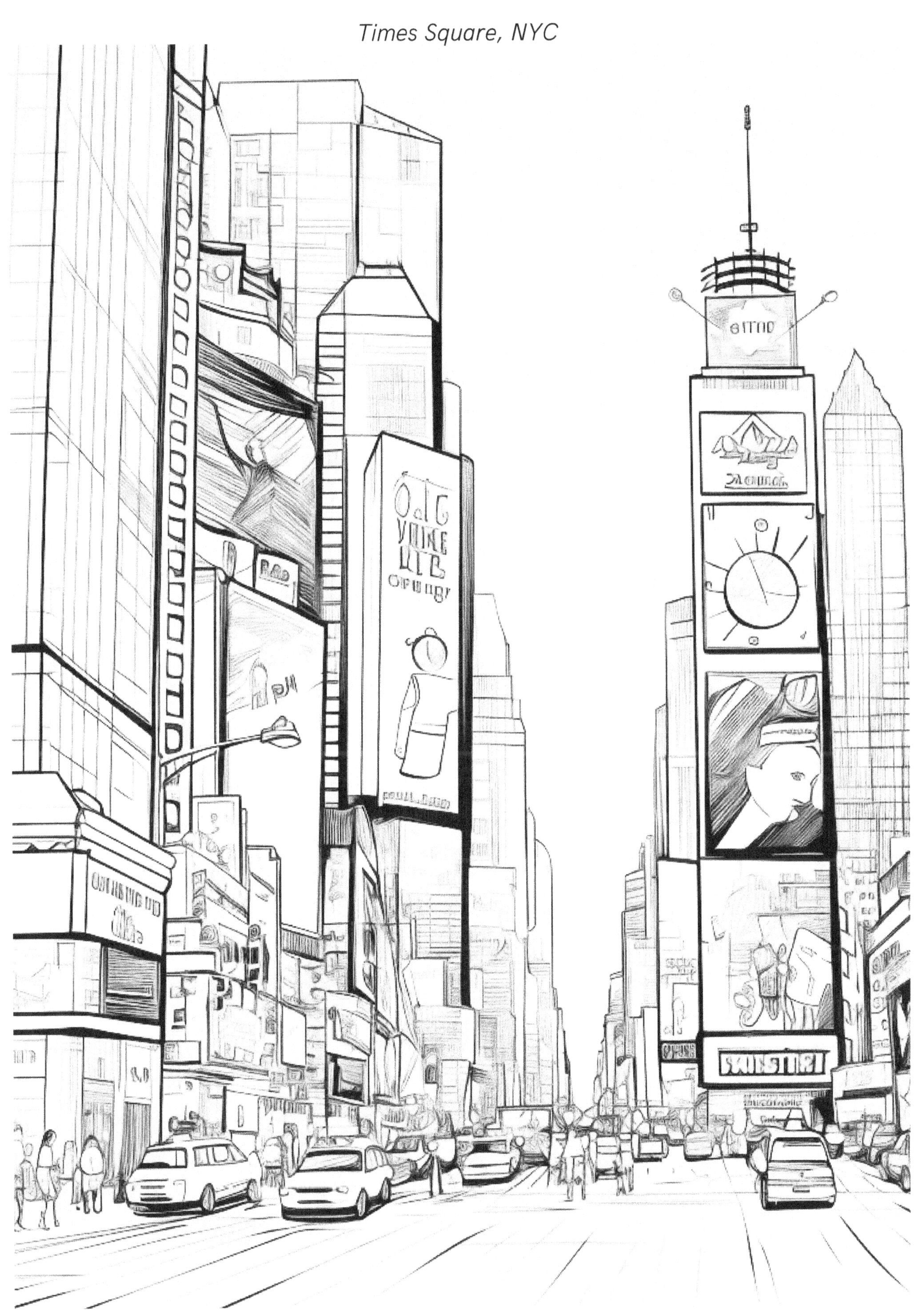

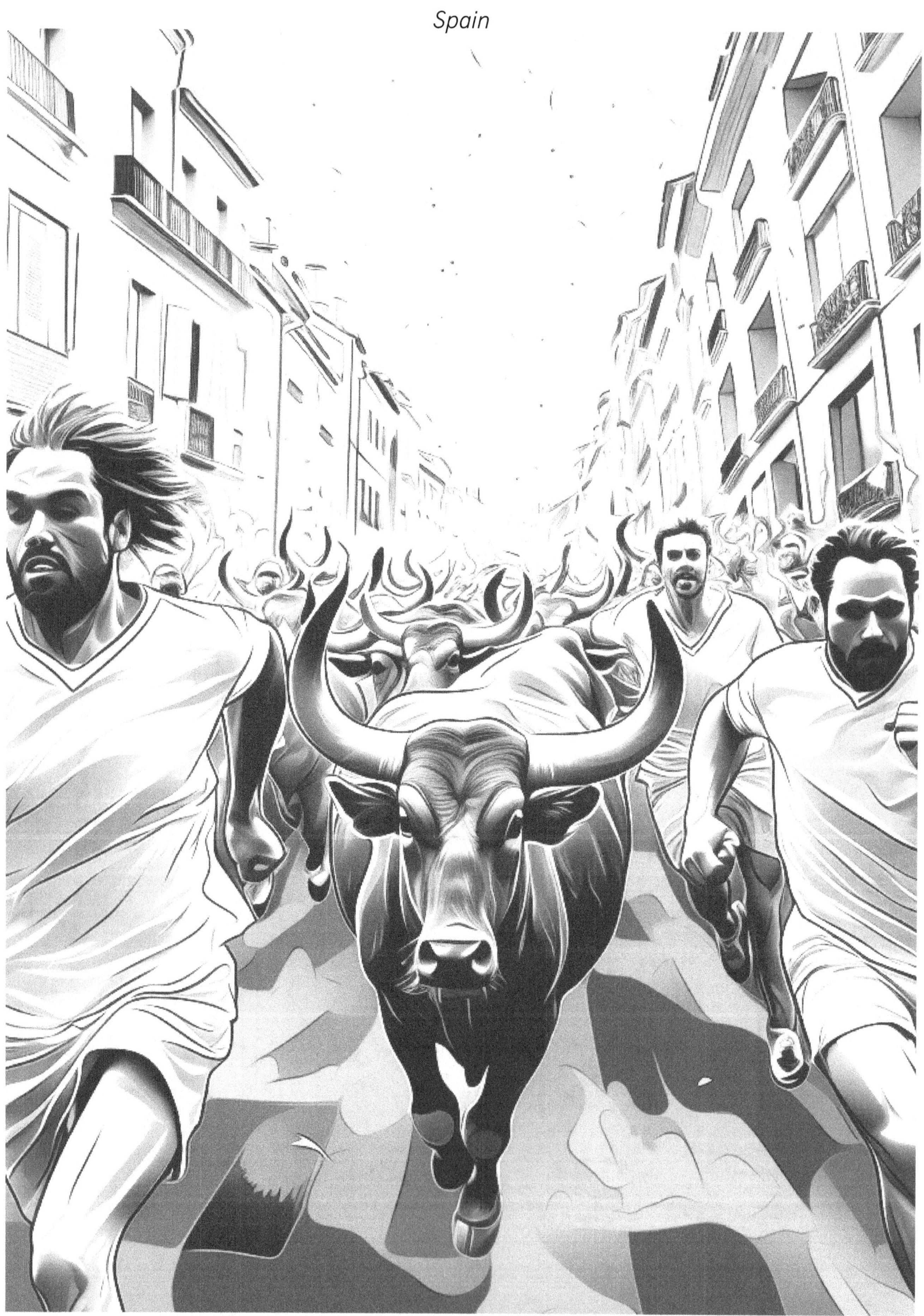

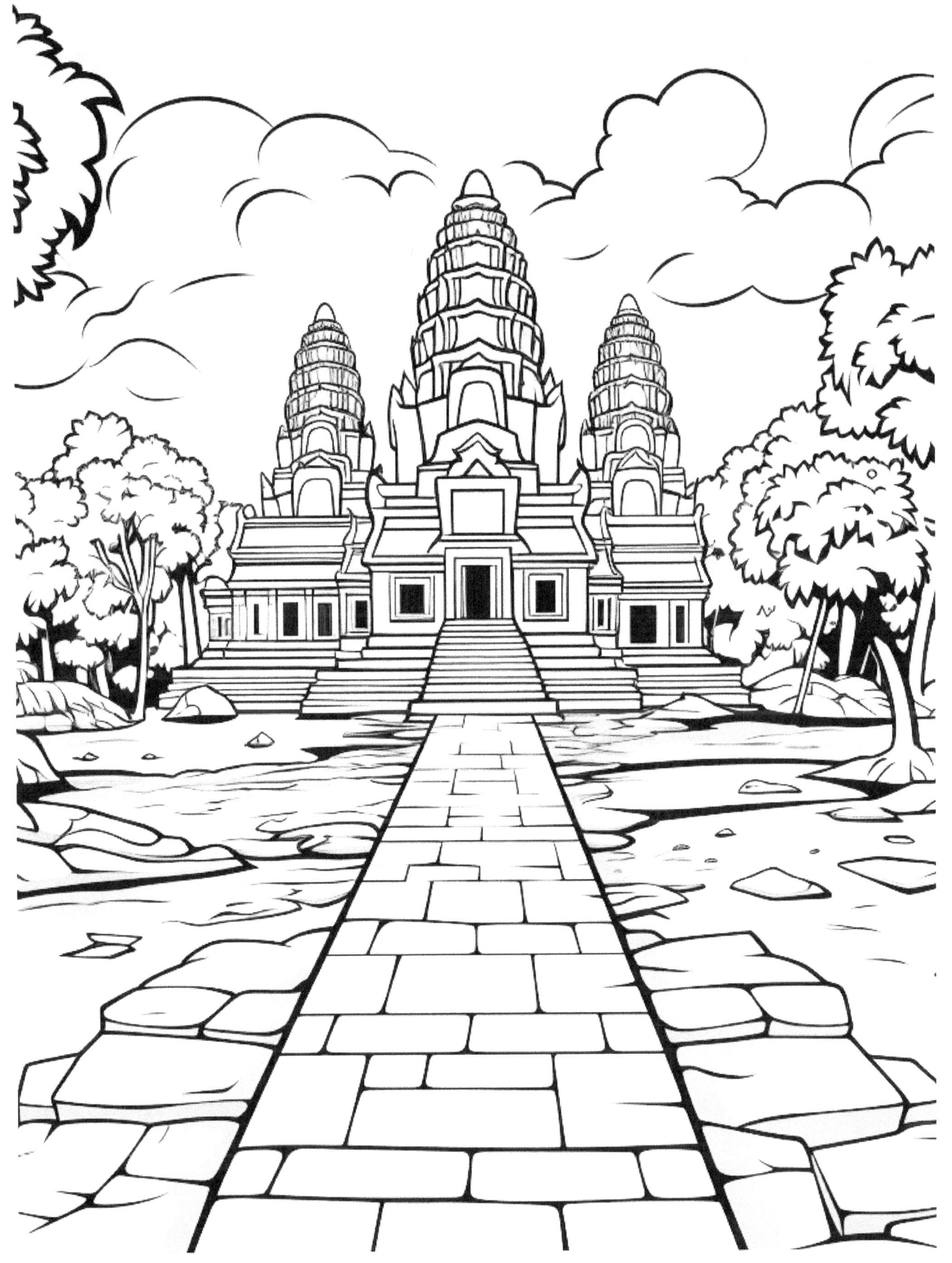
Cambodia

London, UK

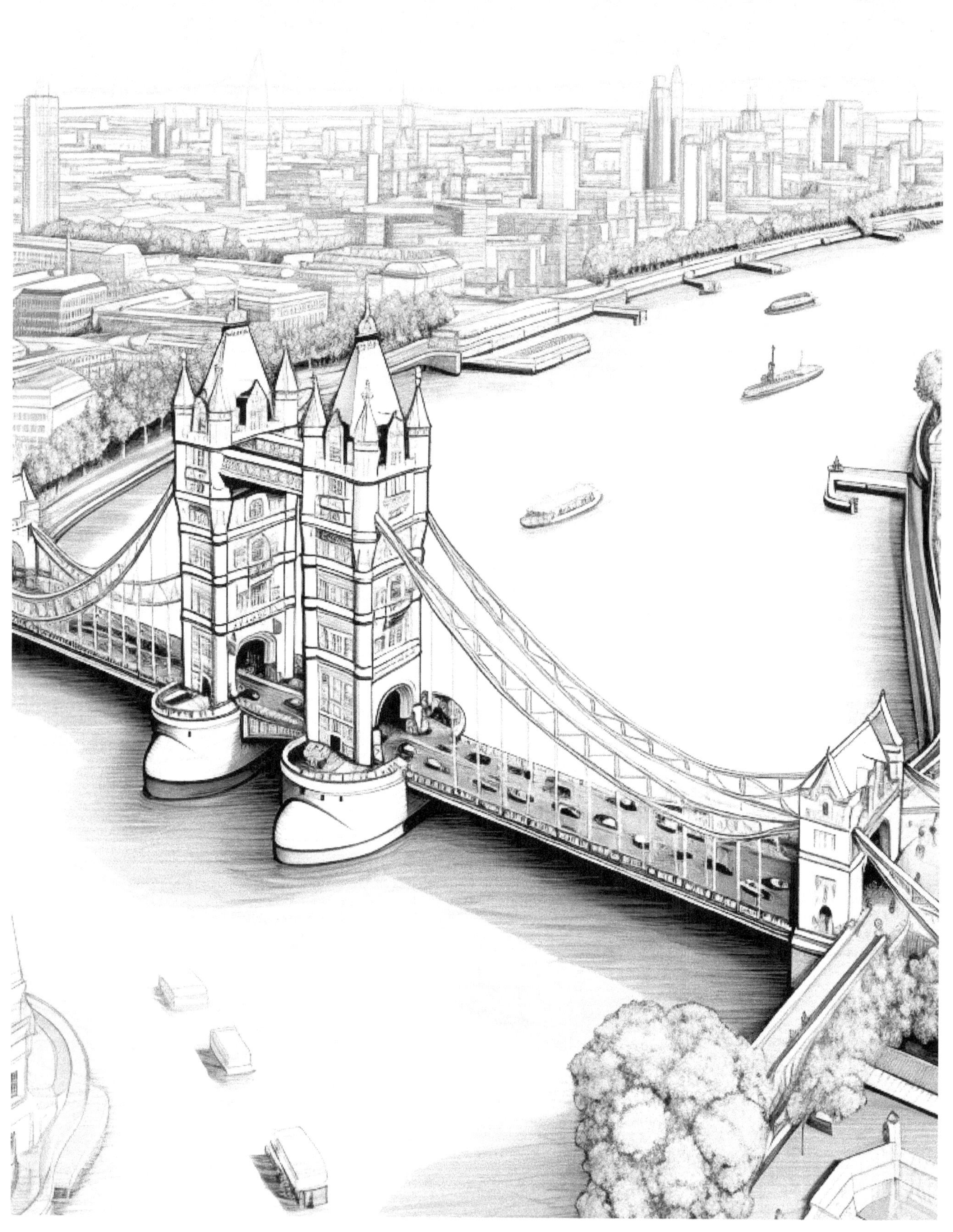

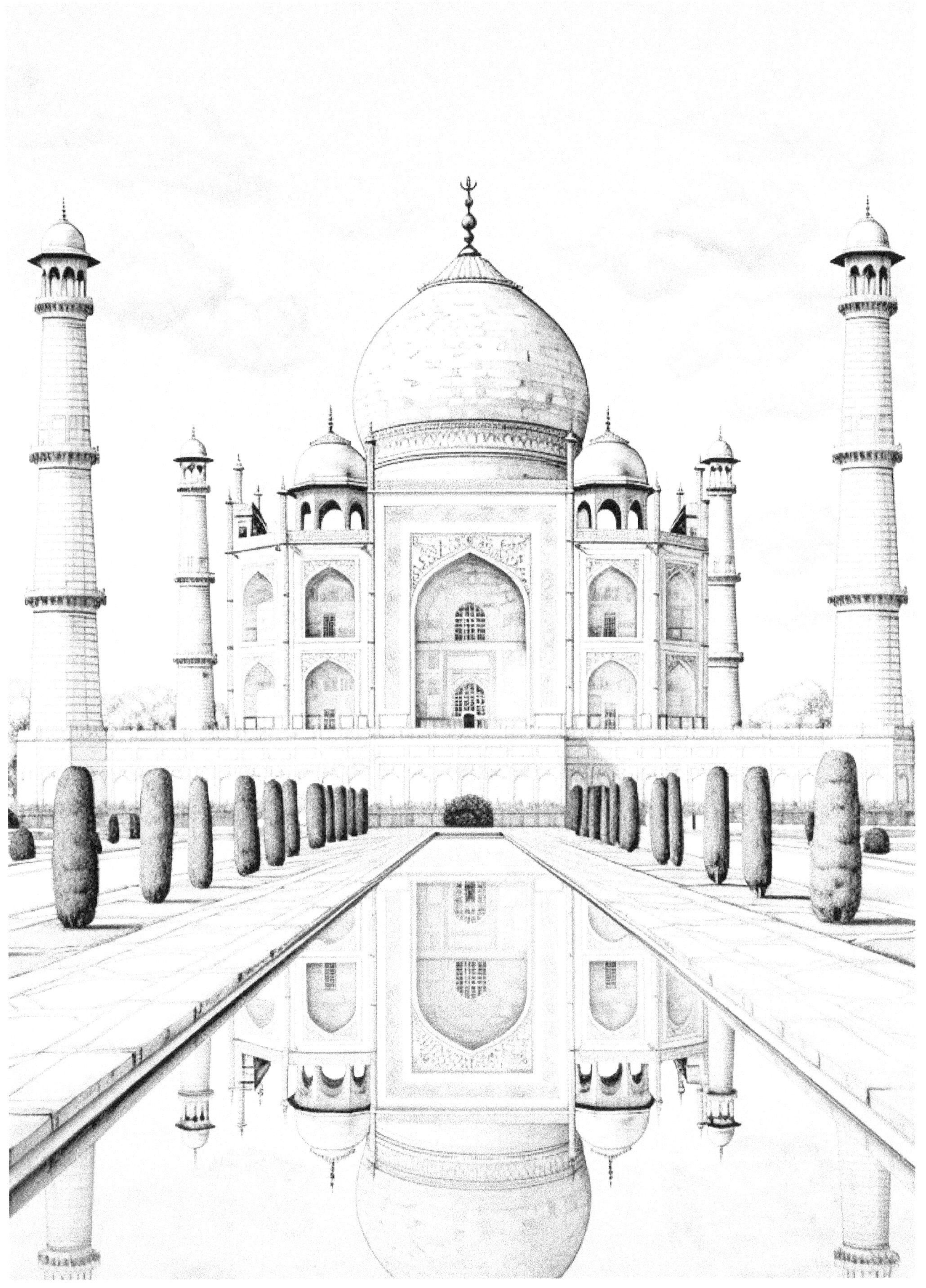

Taj Mahal, India

Native Peruvian Woman

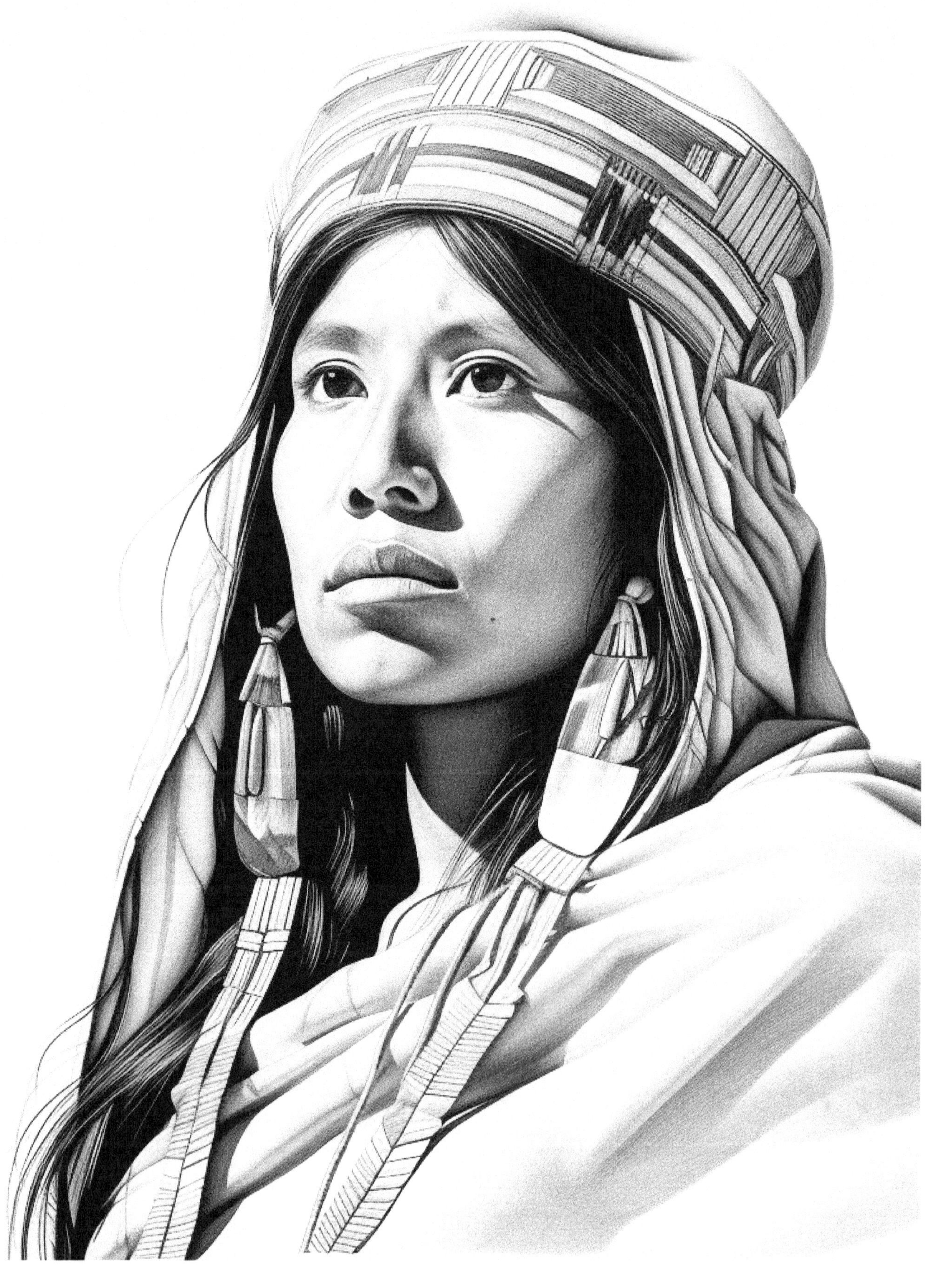

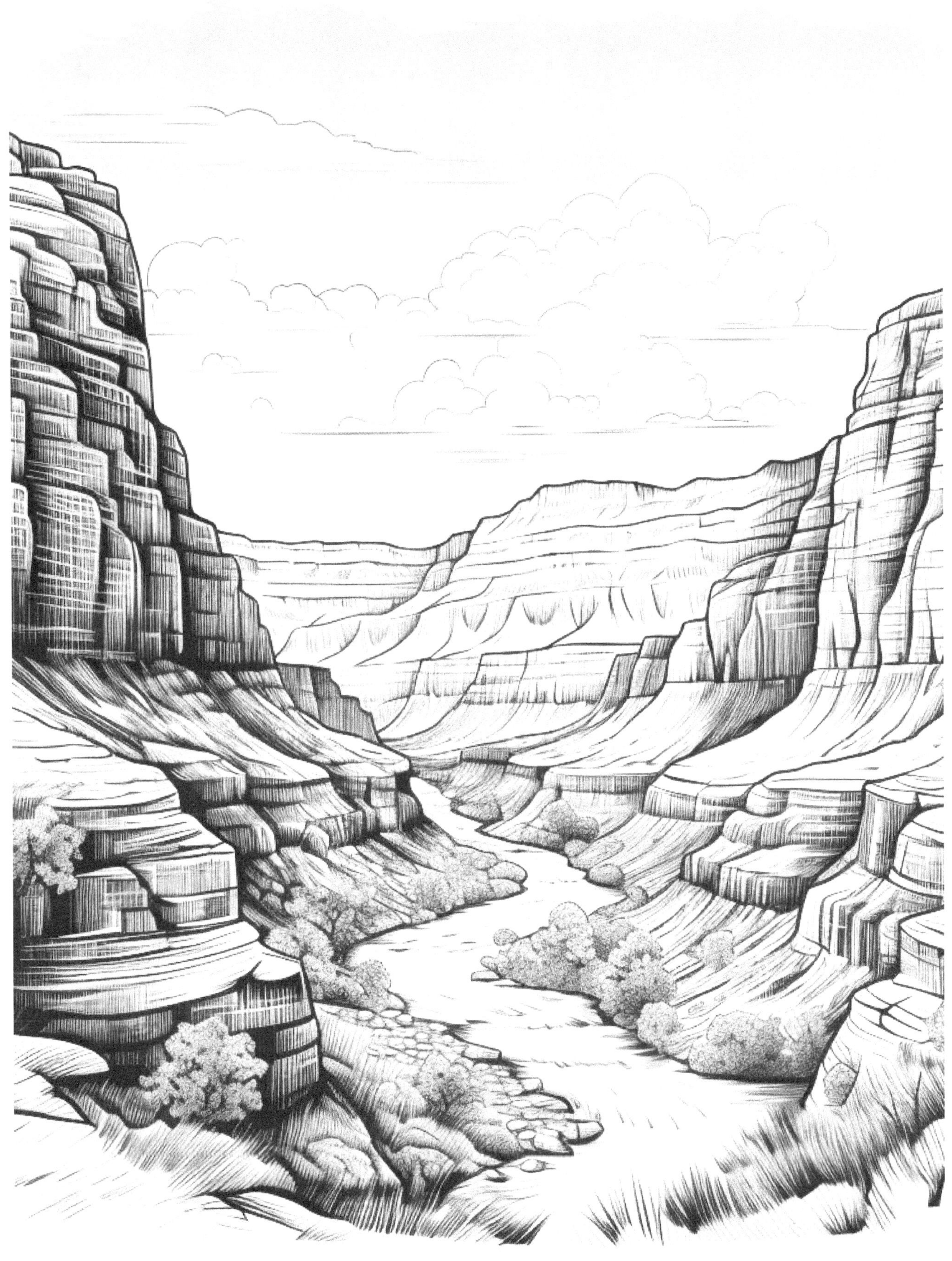

Grand Canyon, Arizona

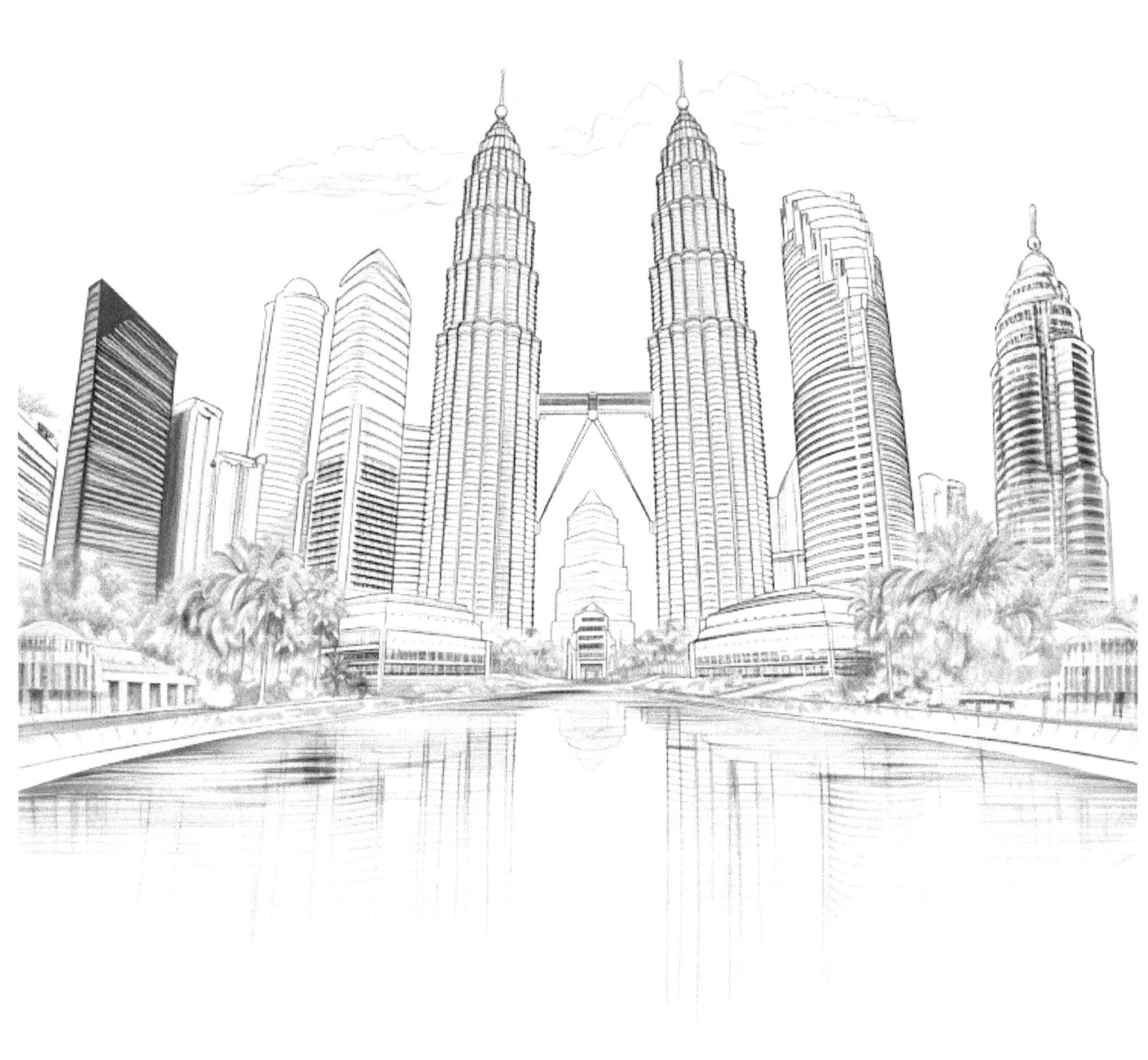
Kuala Lumpur, Malaysia

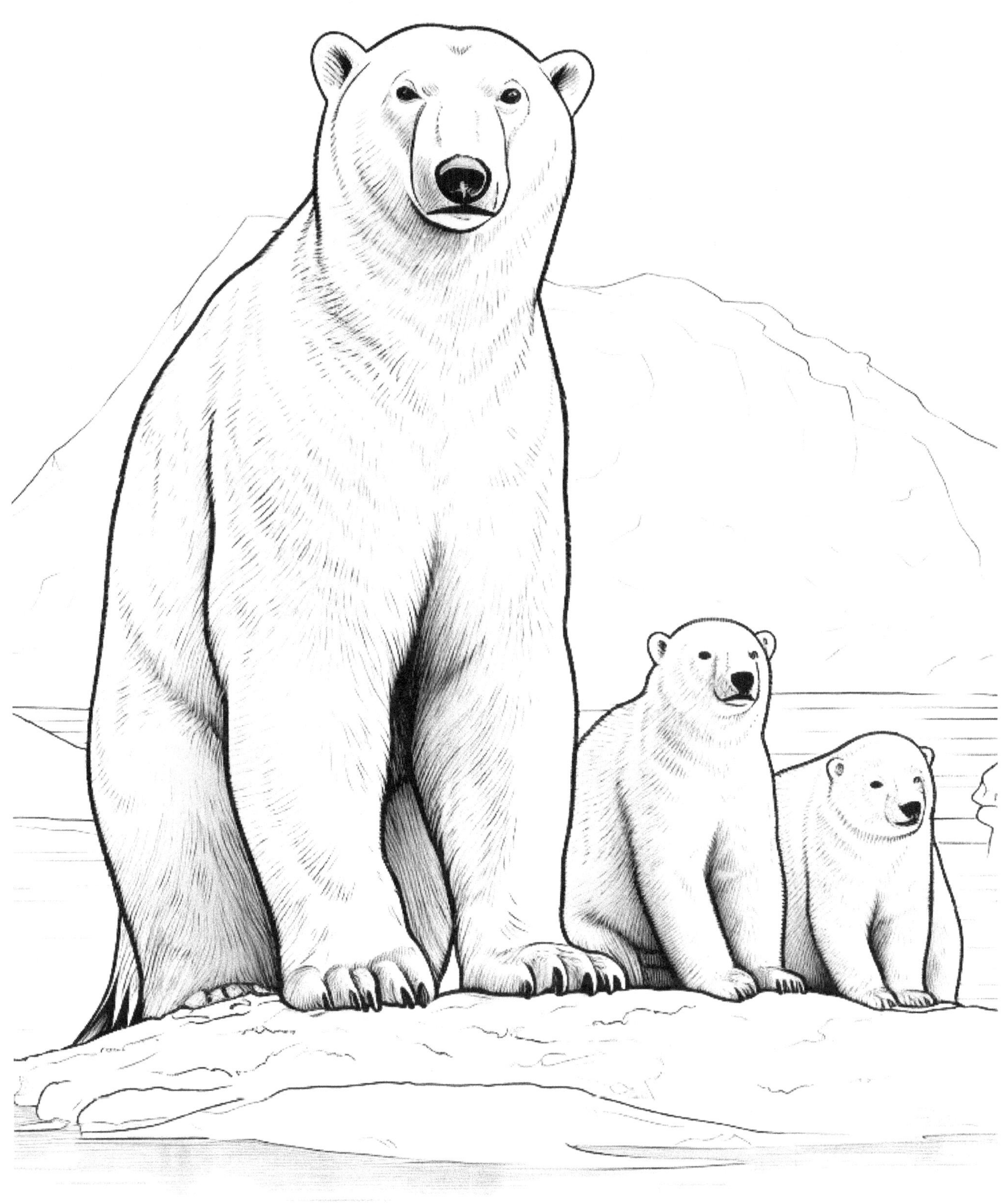

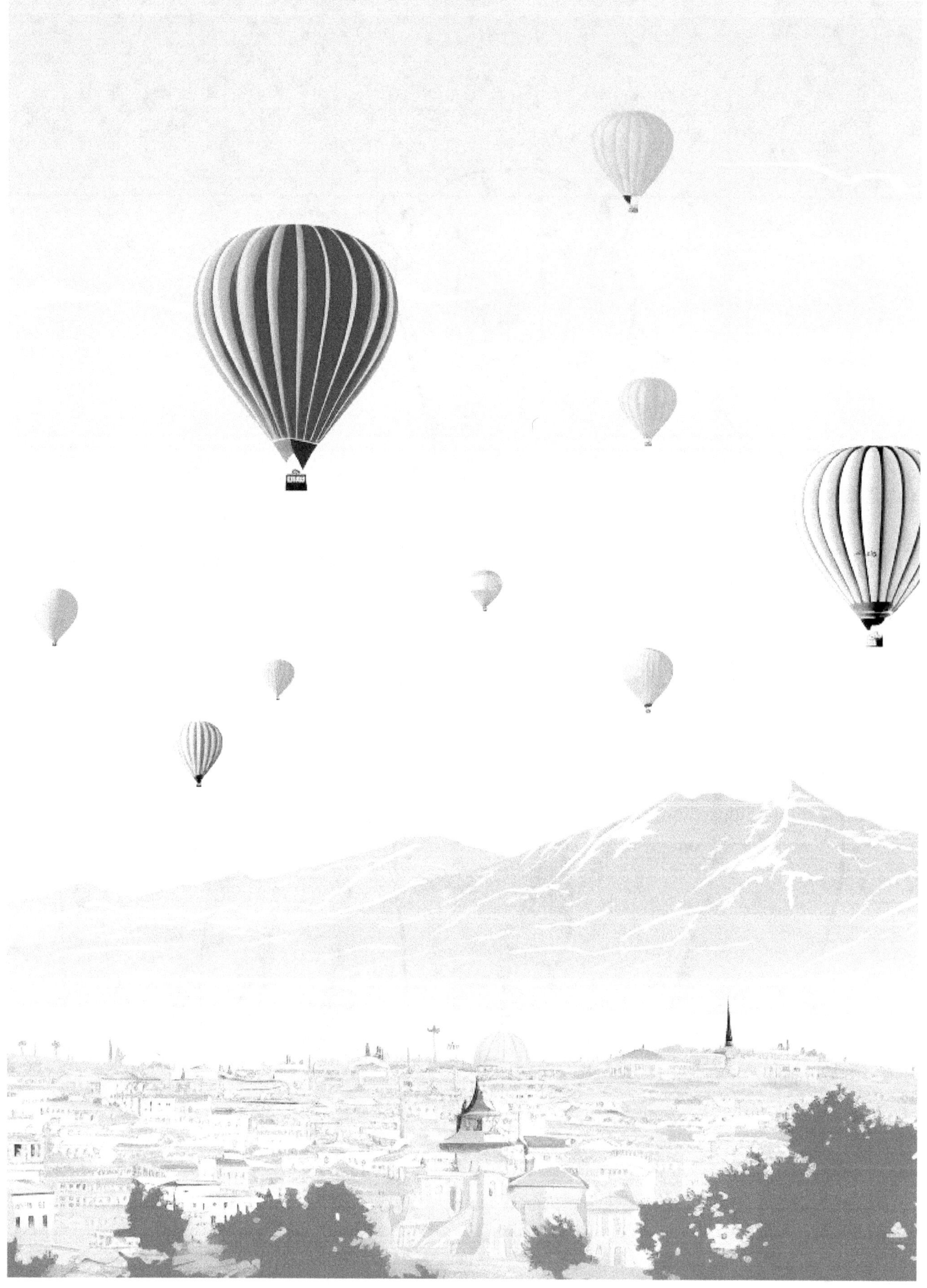

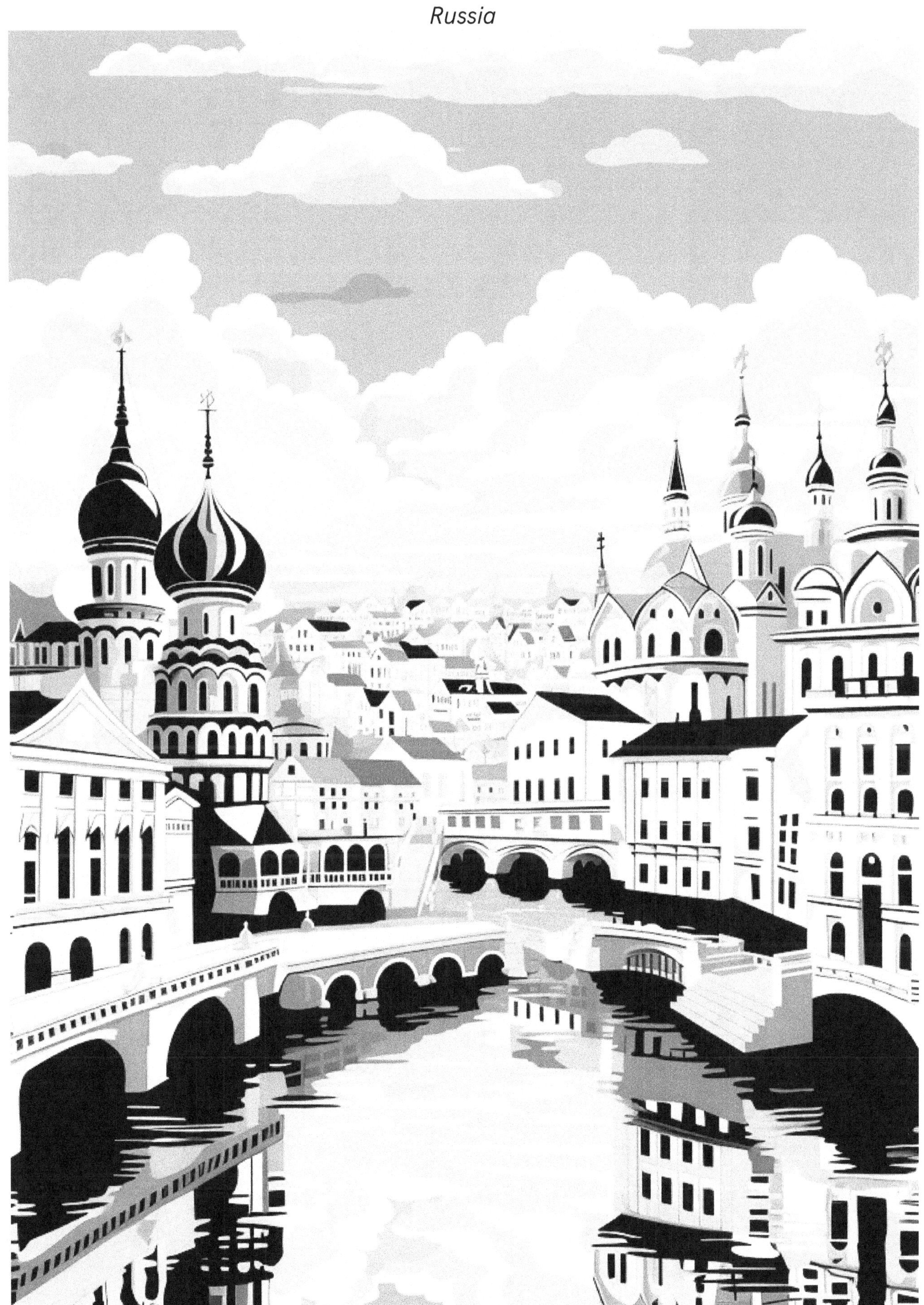

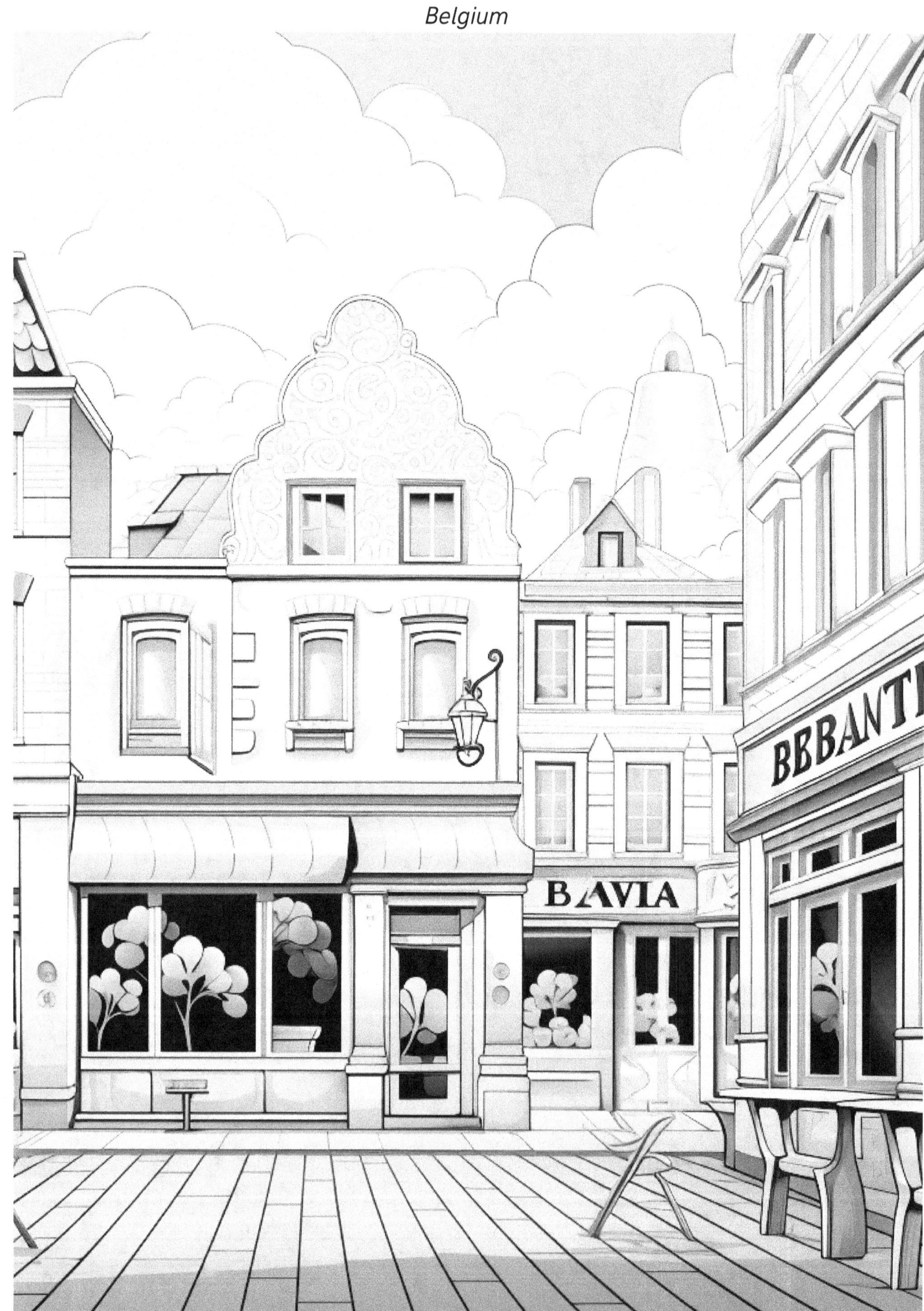
BAVIA
BBANTI

Sloth in Costa Rica

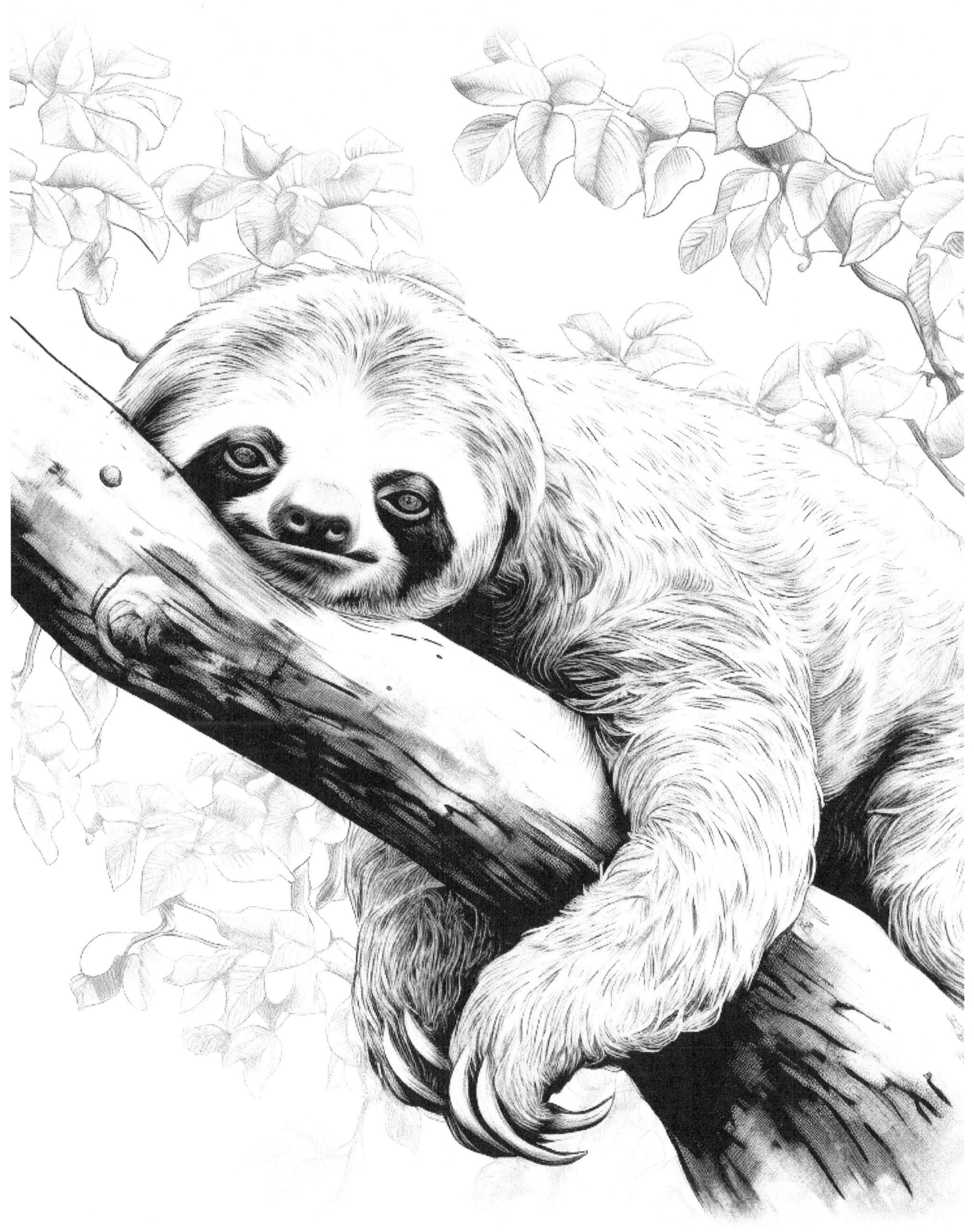

St. Andrews Golf Course, Ireland

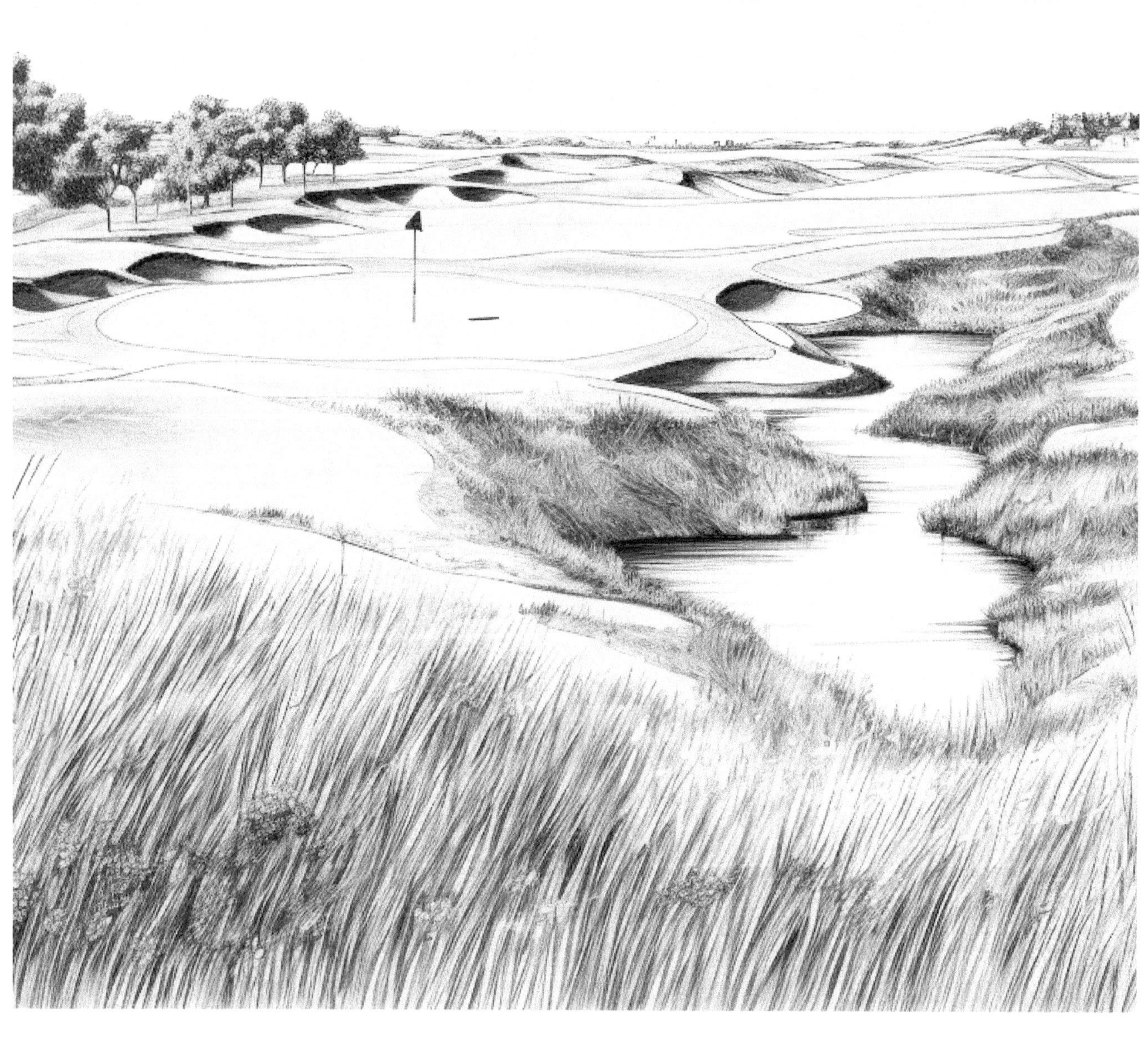

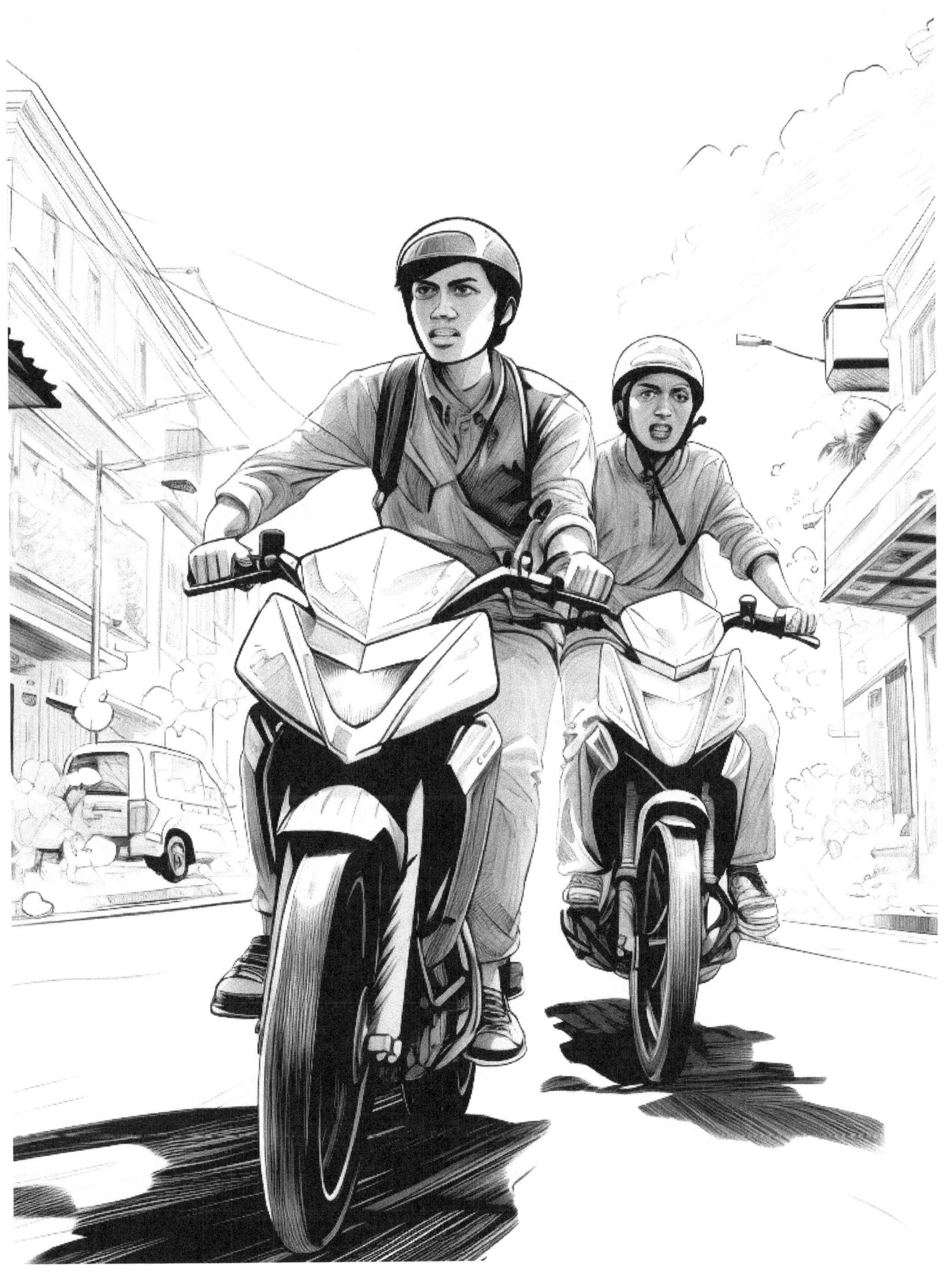

Thailand

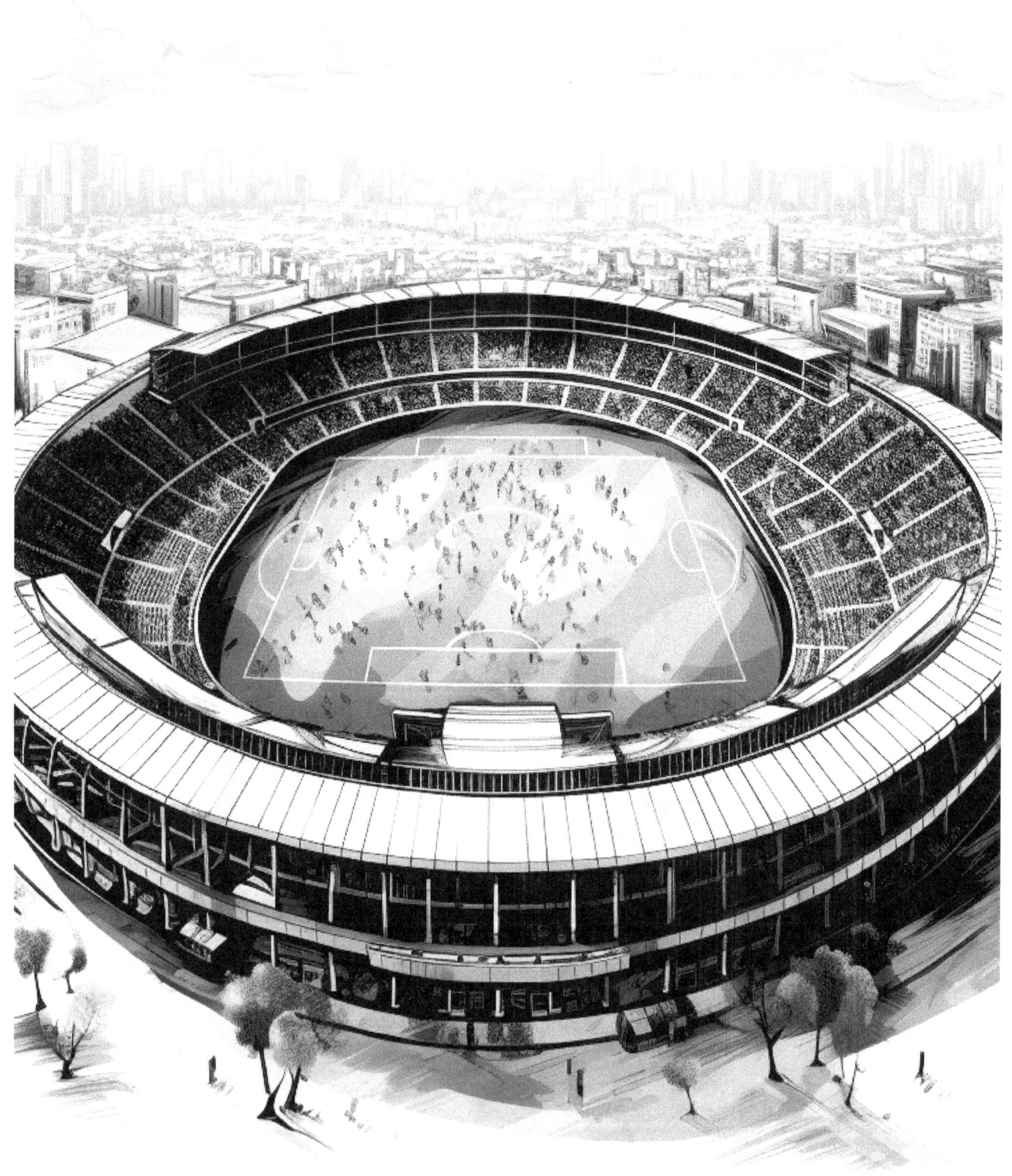

Brazil

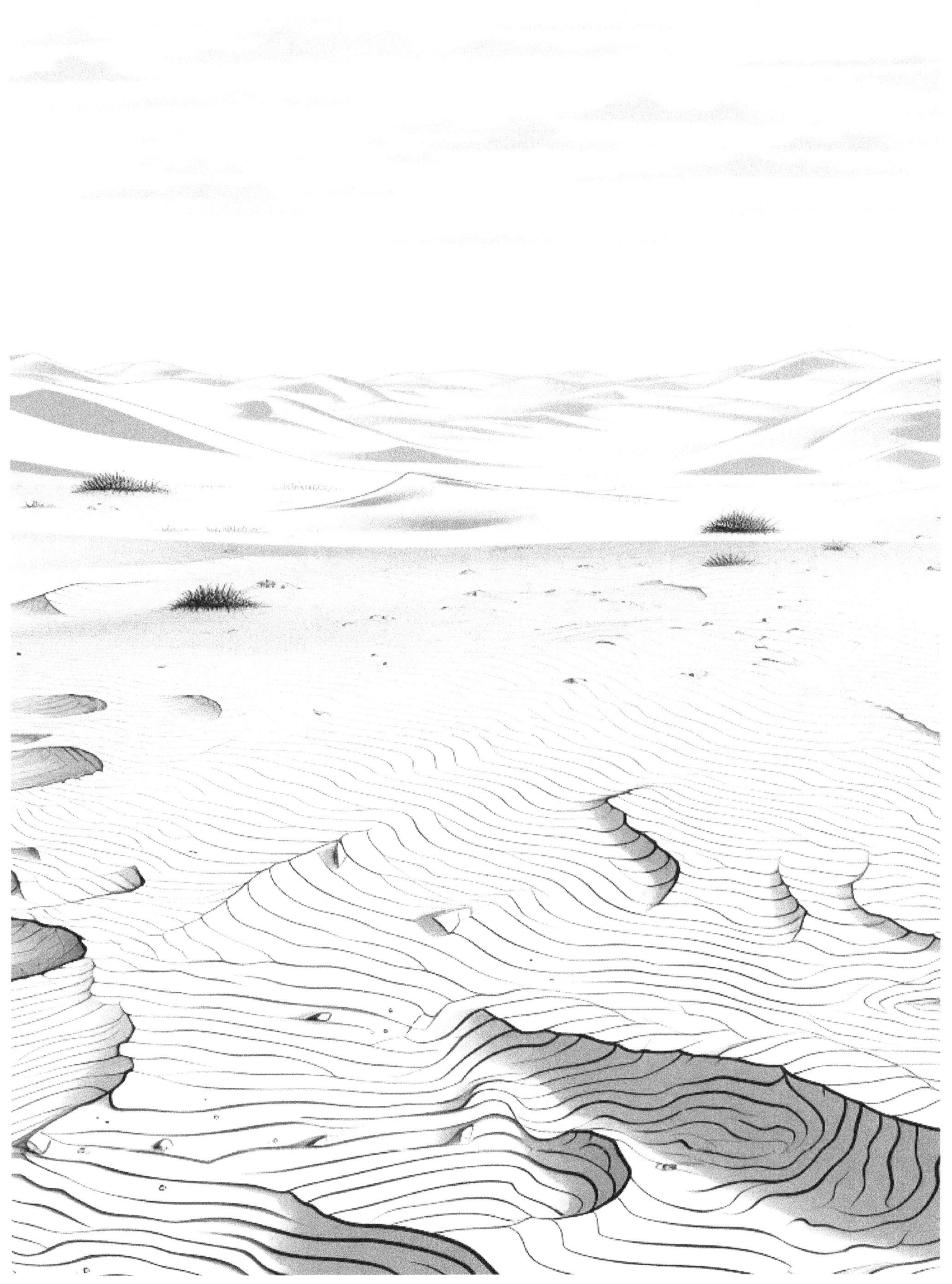

Namib Desert, Namibia

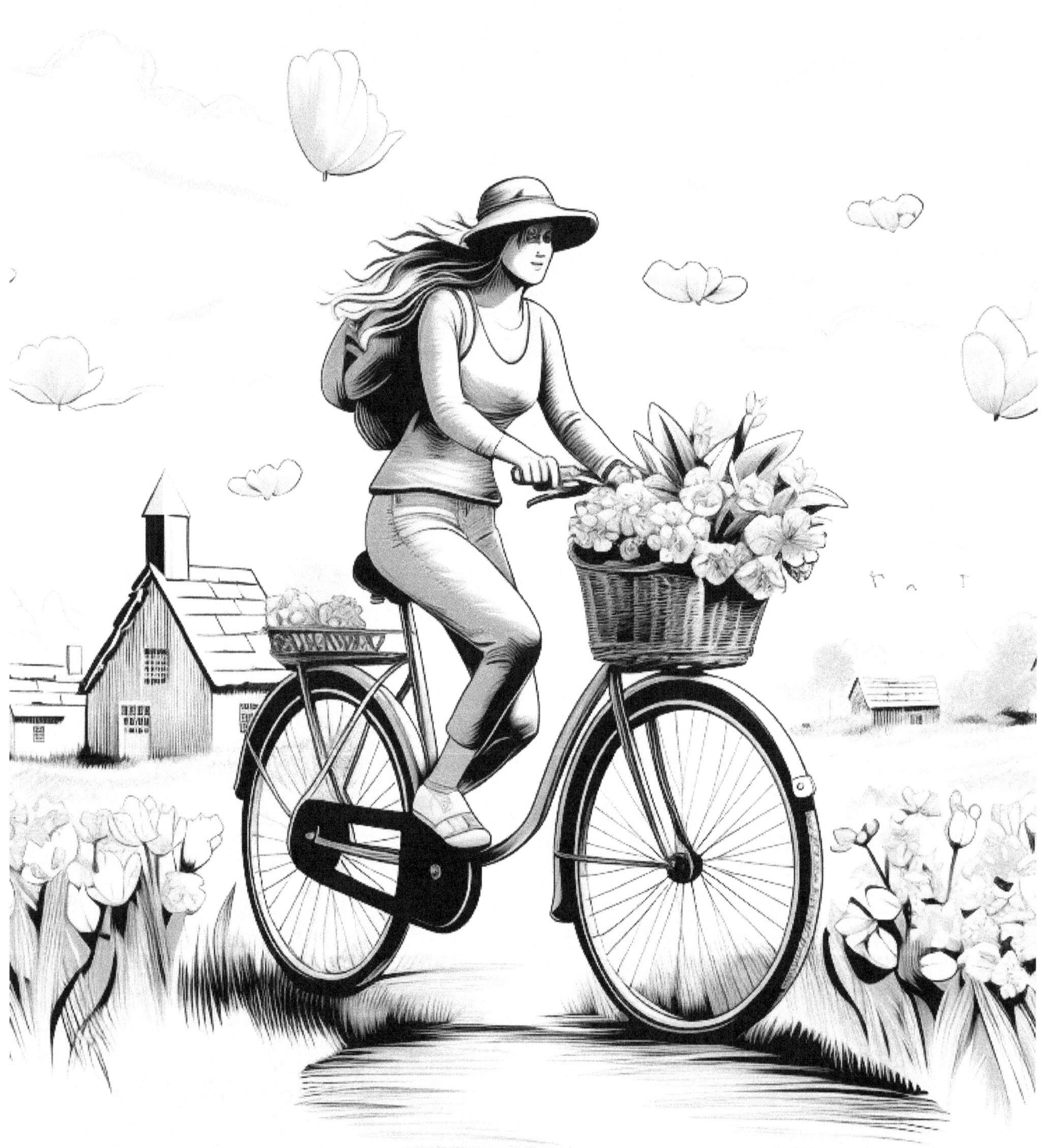

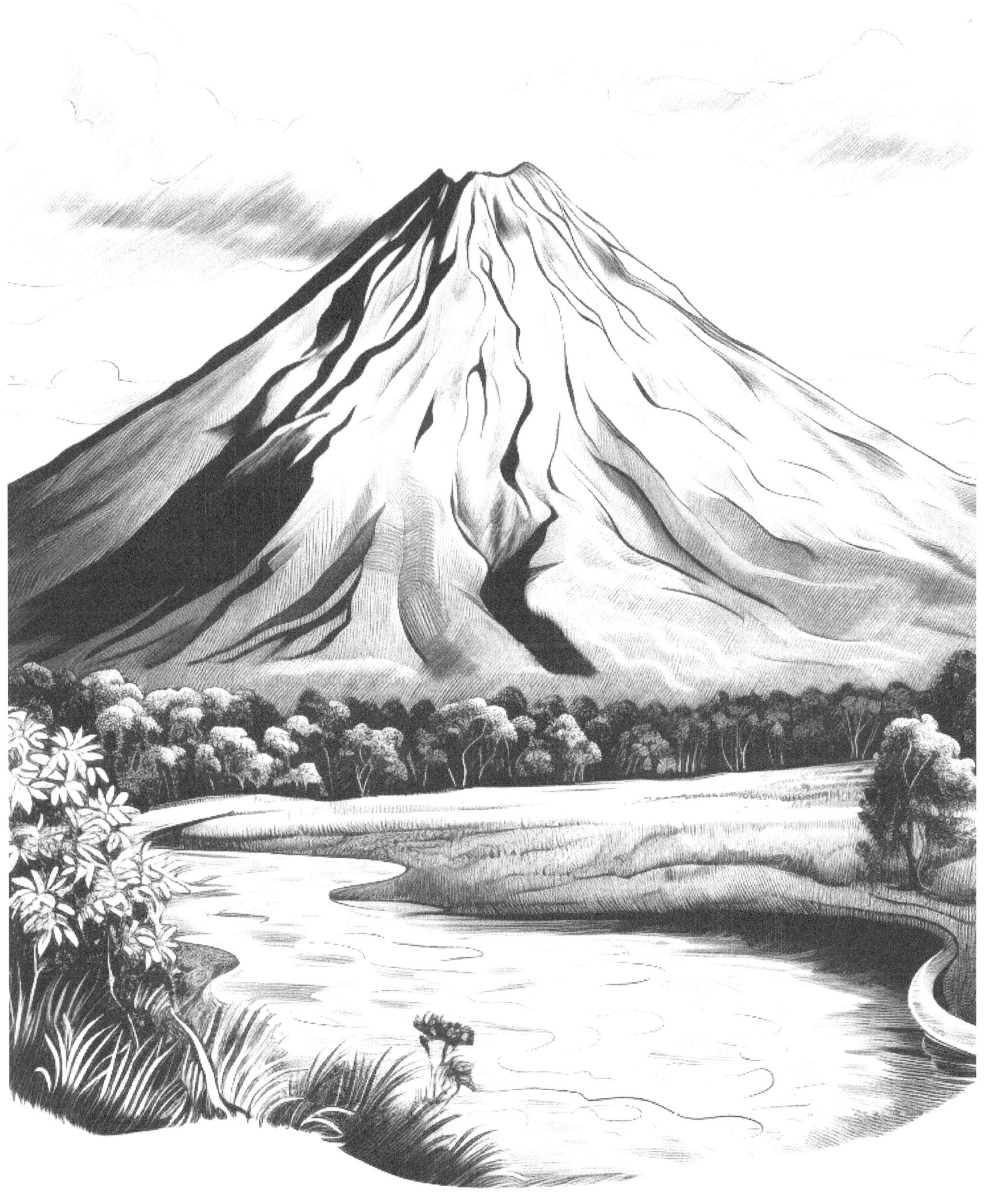

Arenal Volcano, Costa Rica

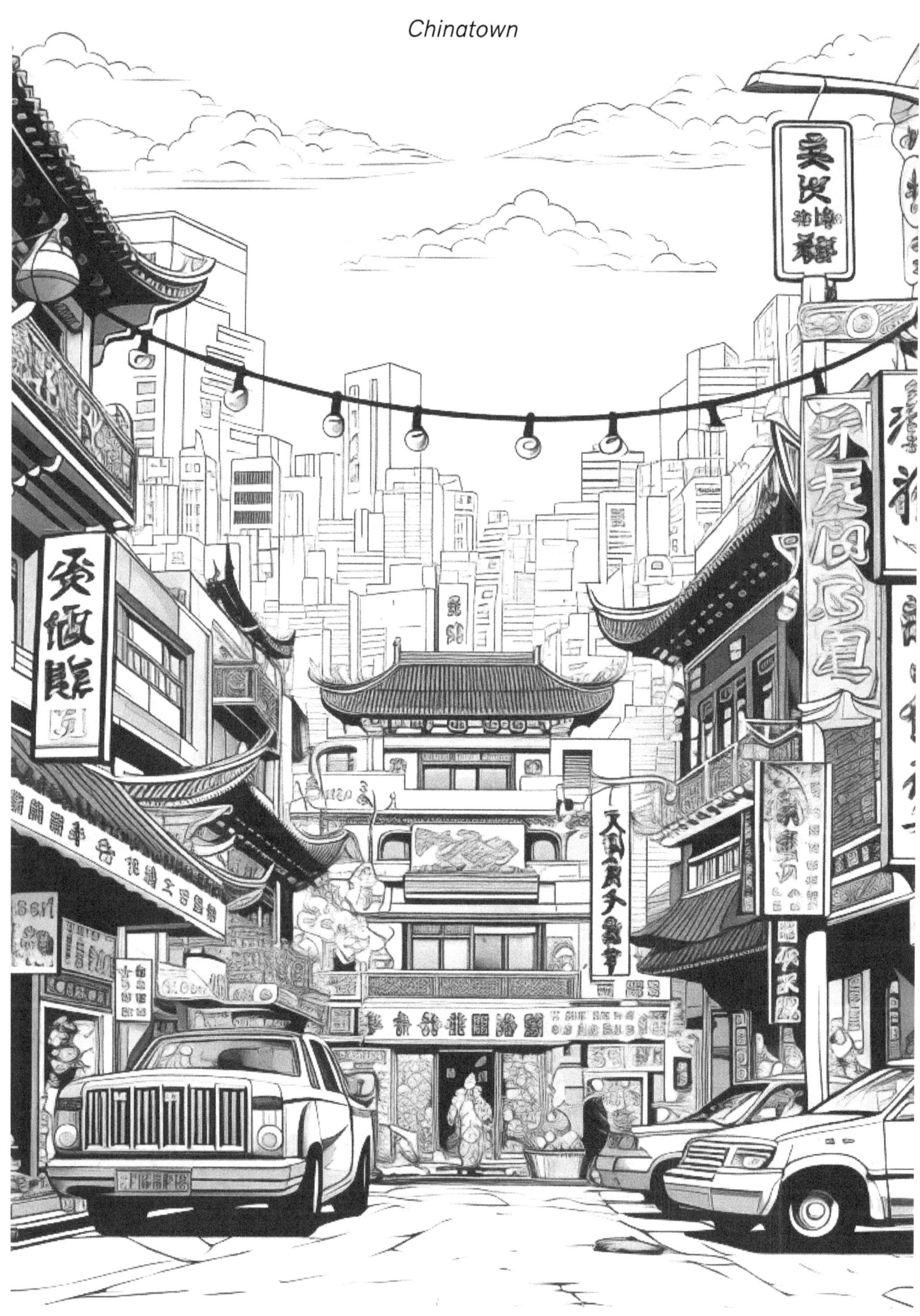

Samoan Rugby Player

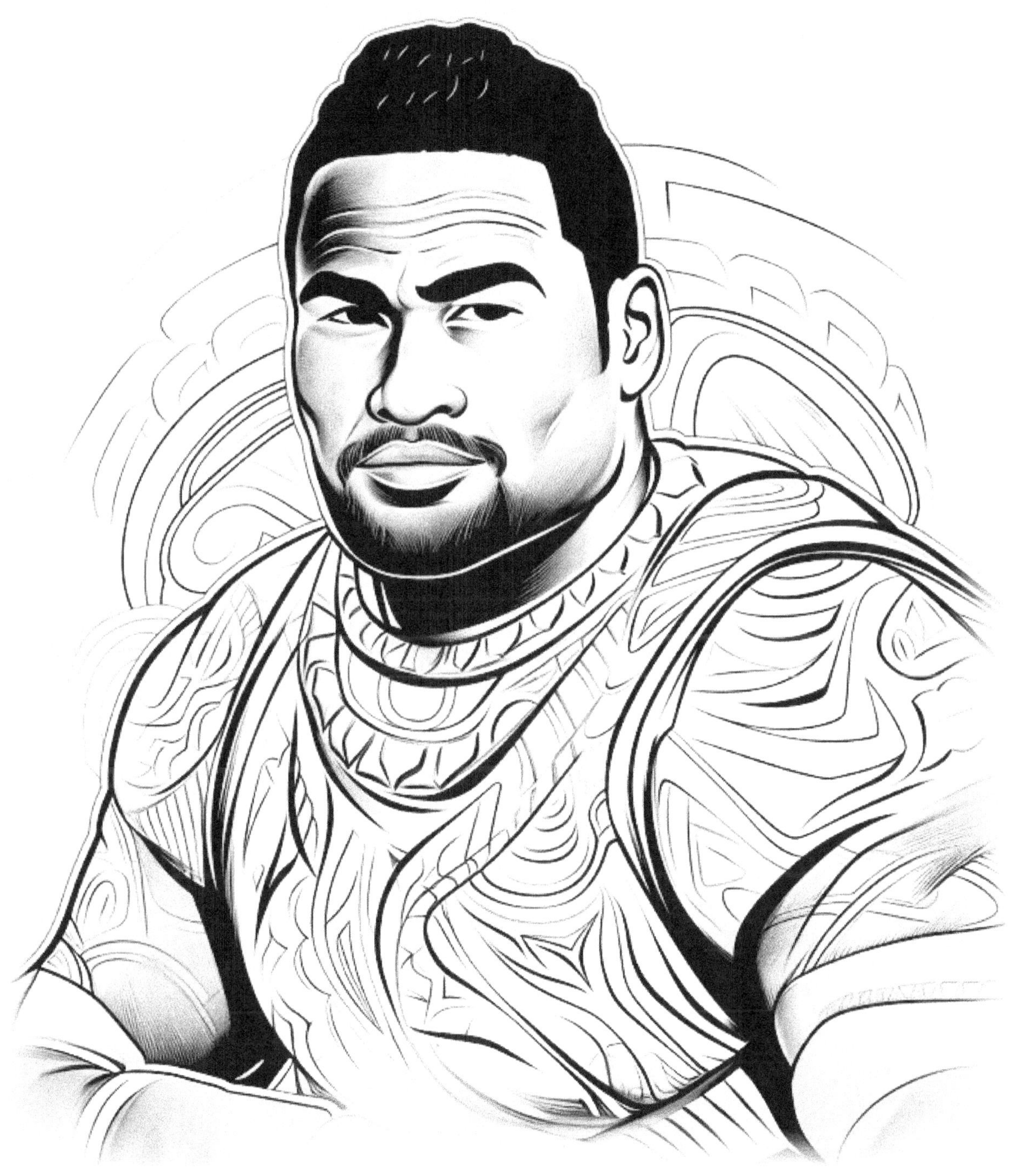

Victoria Falls, Zambia

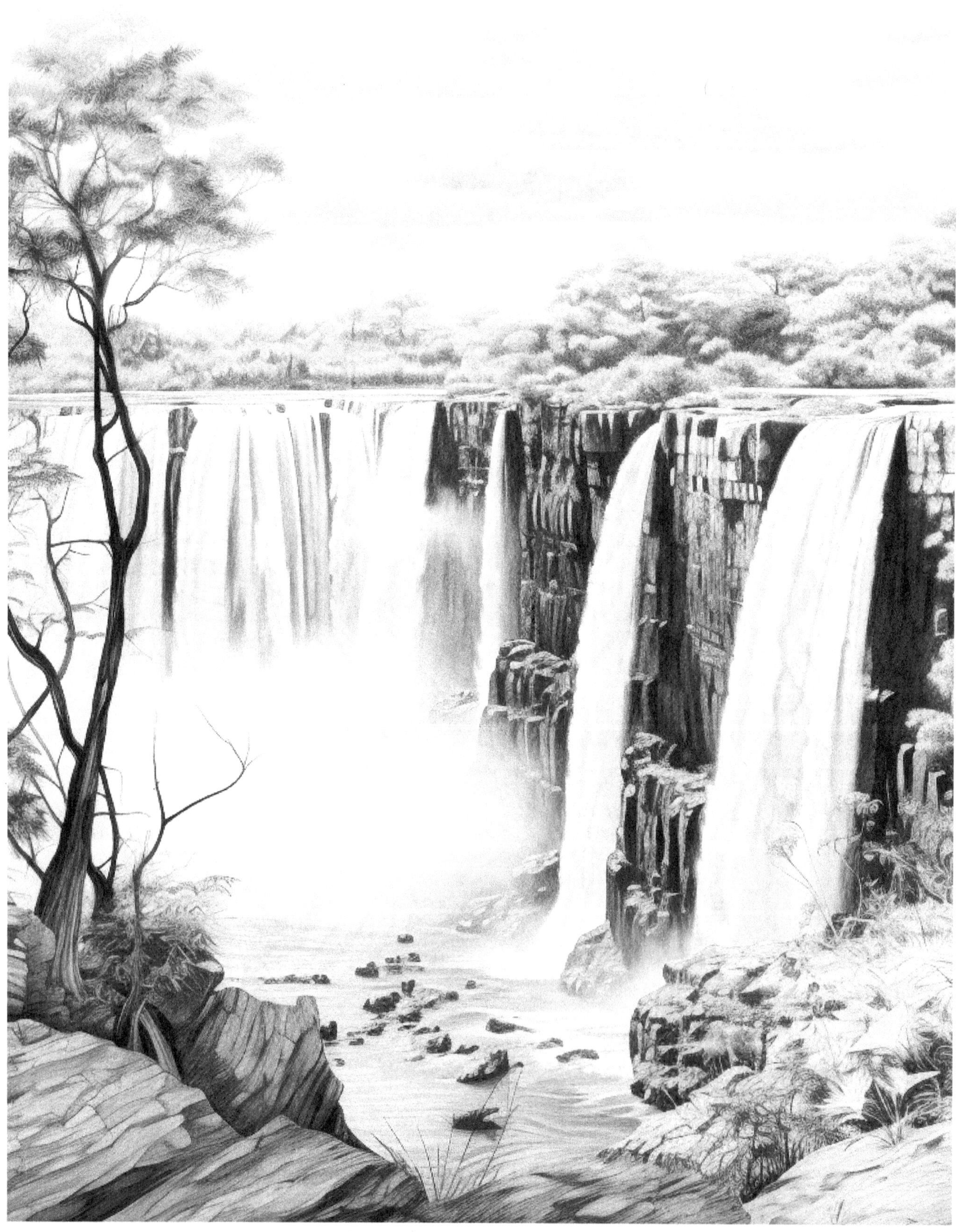

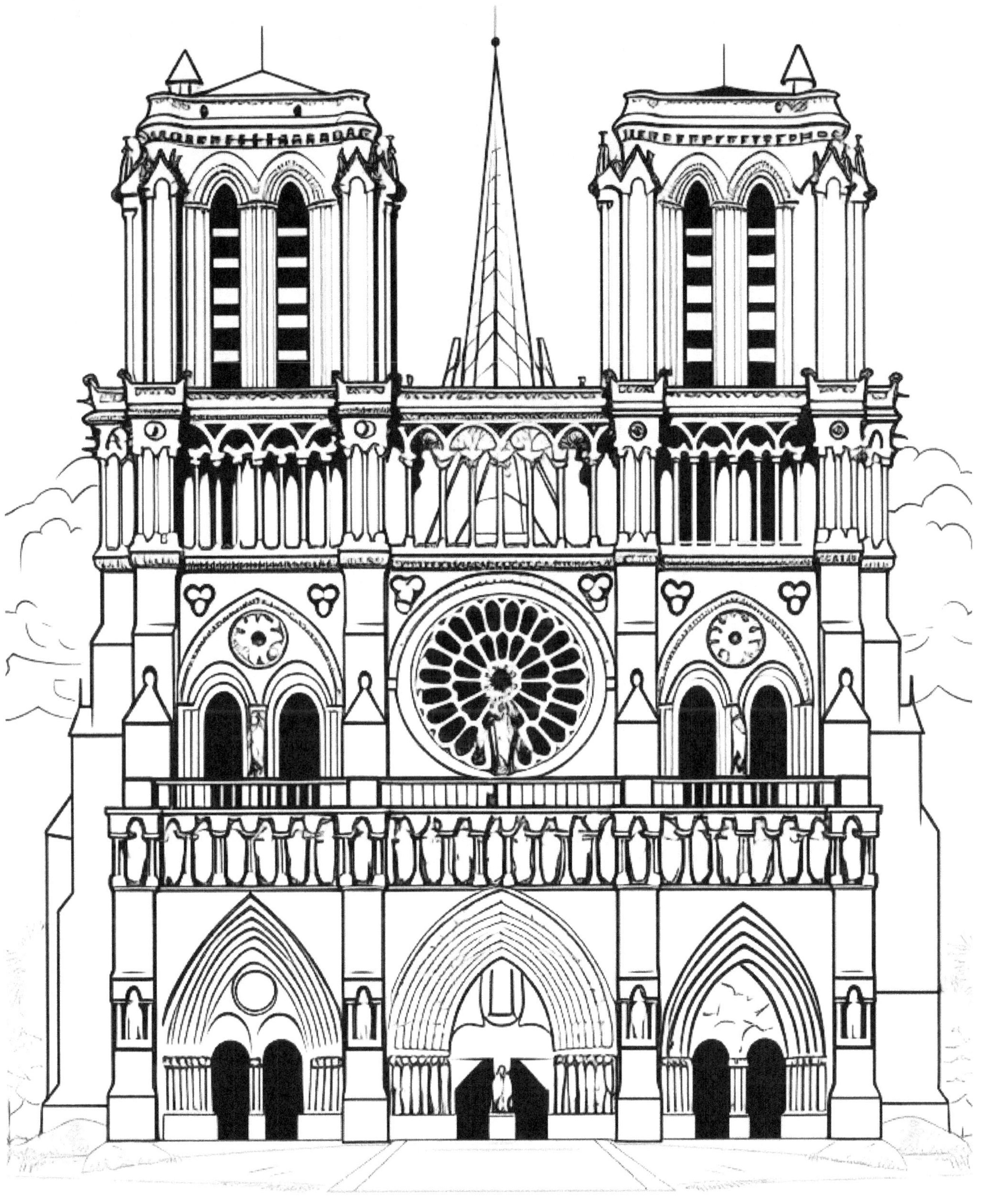

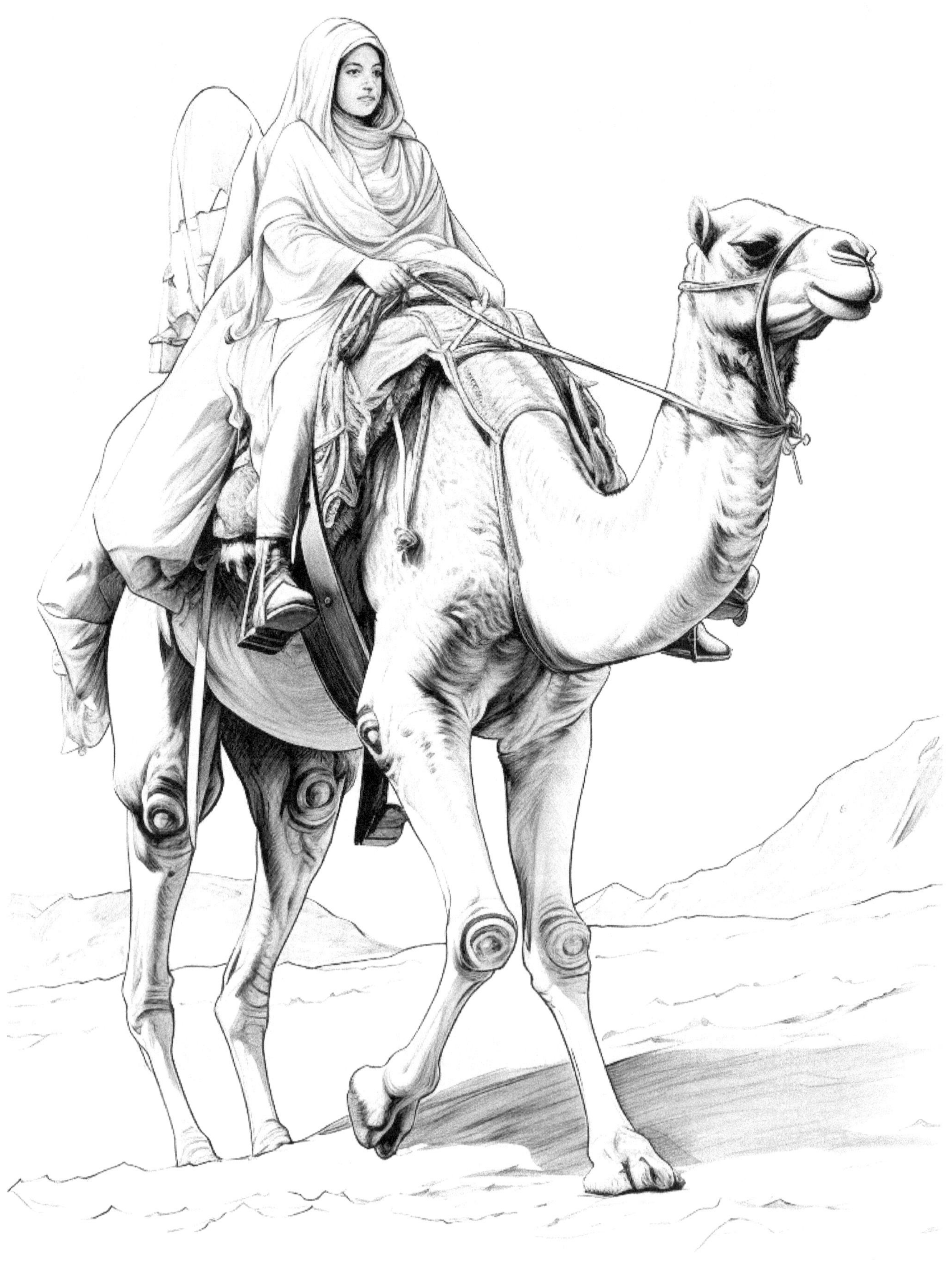

Morocco

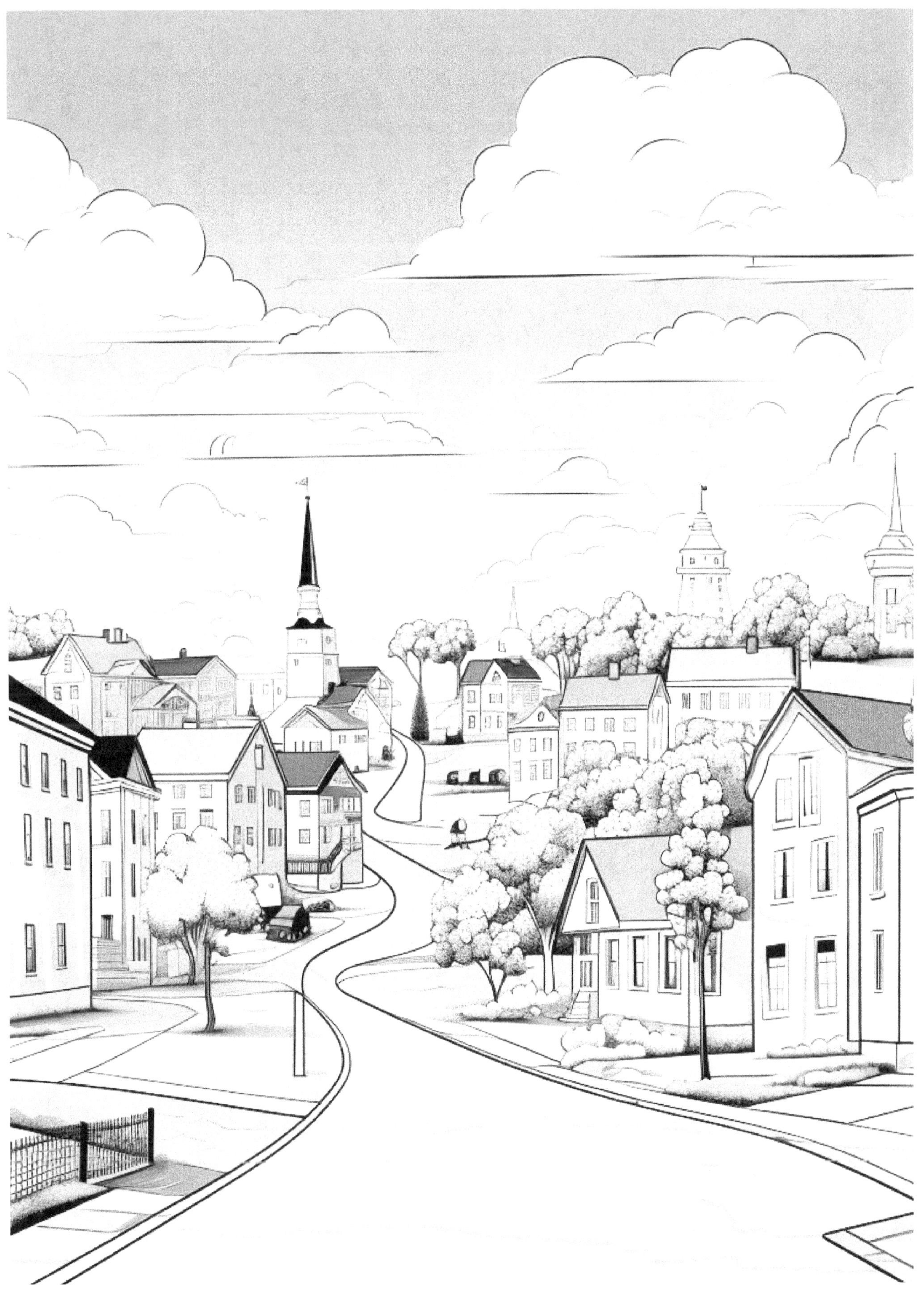
Sweden

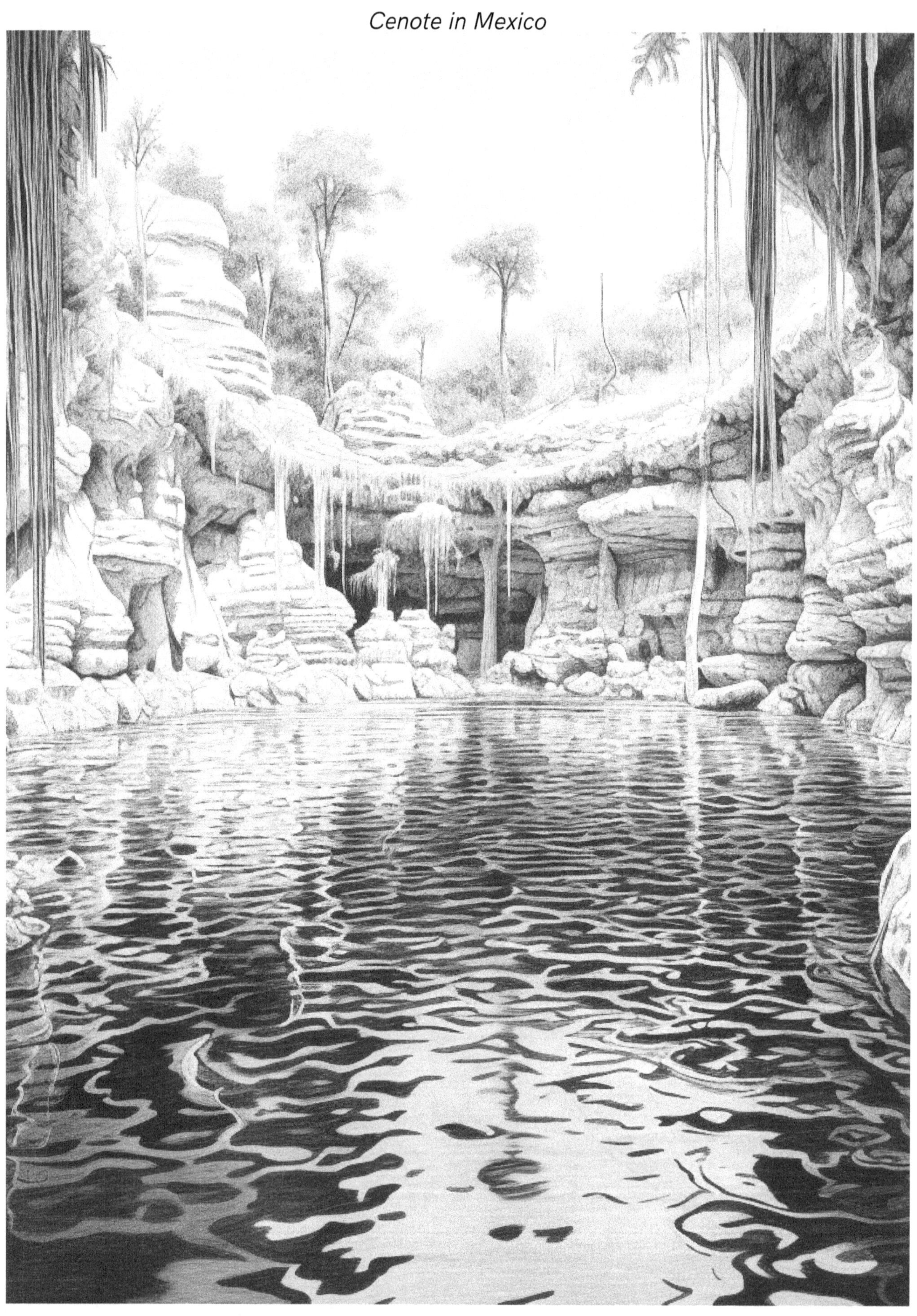

Cenote in Mexico

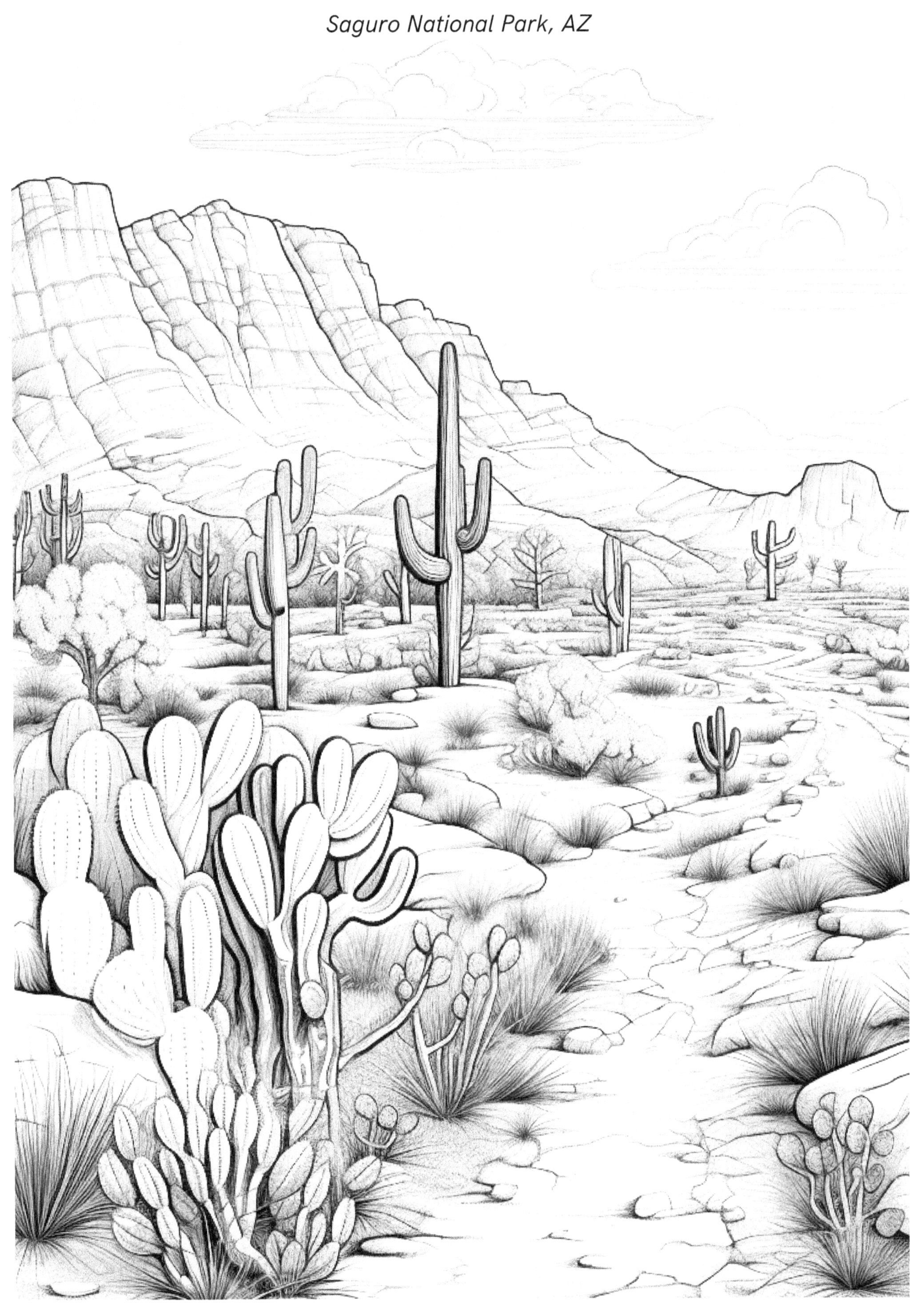

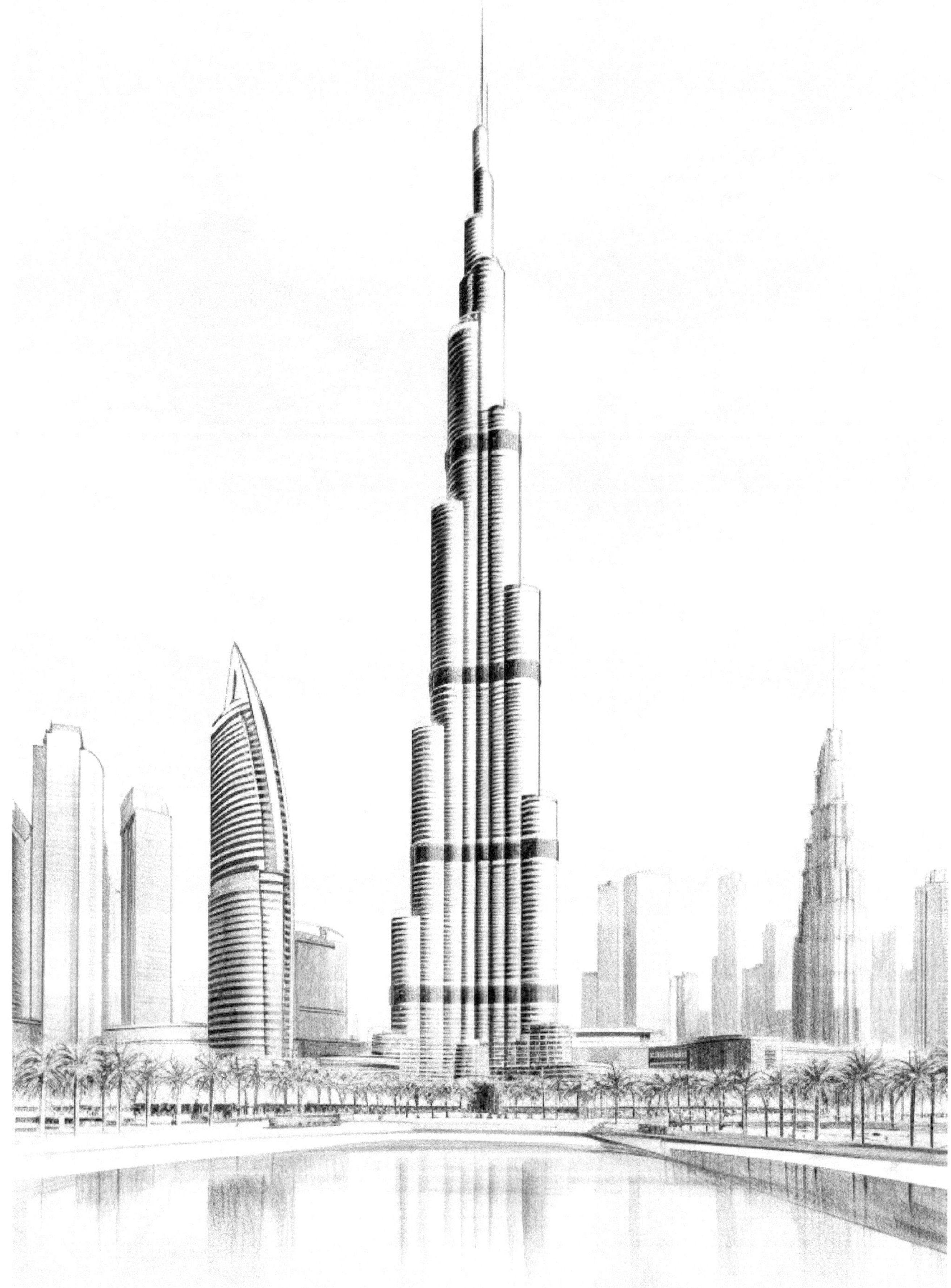

Dubai, UAE

Milan, Italy

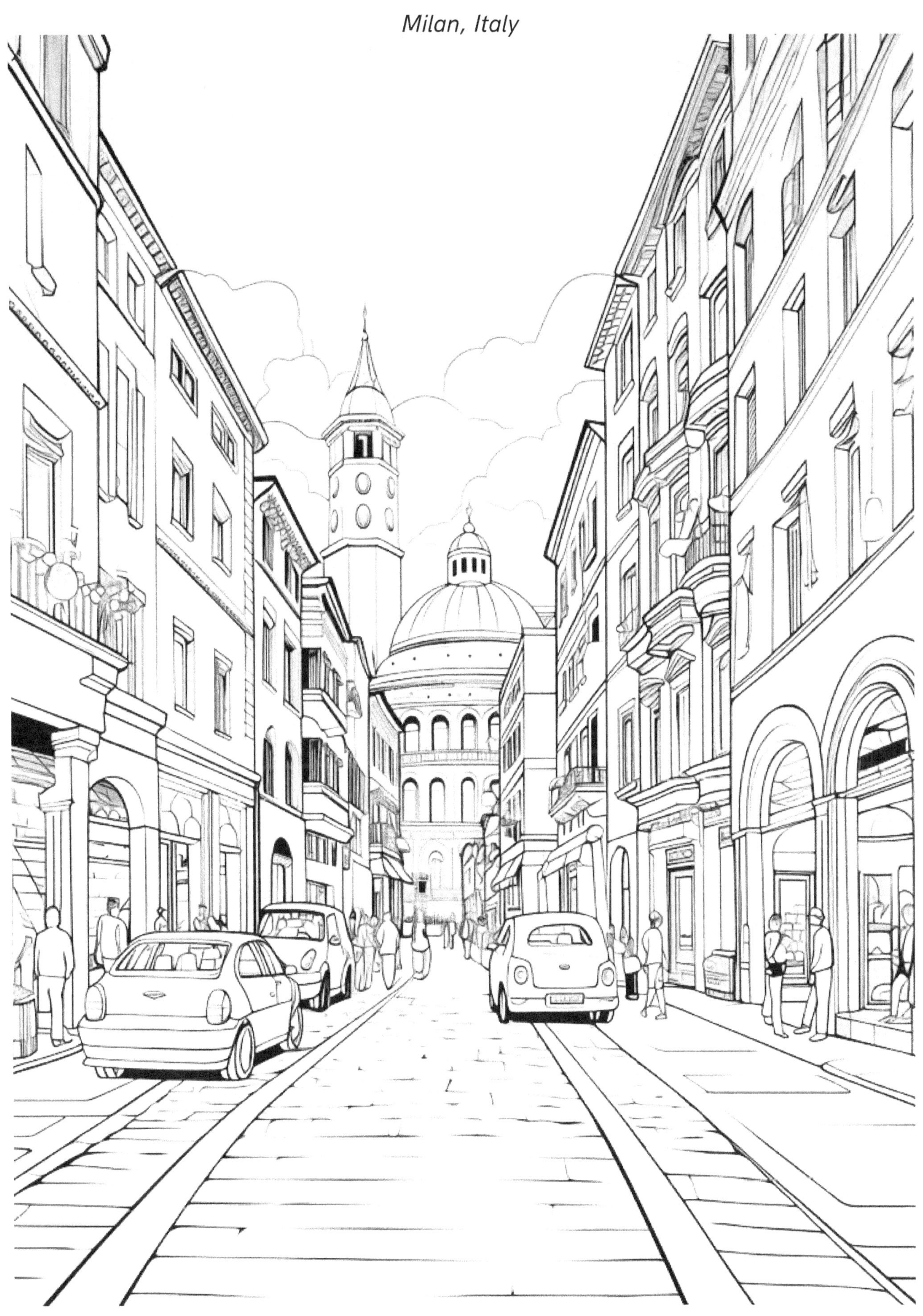

Northern Lights

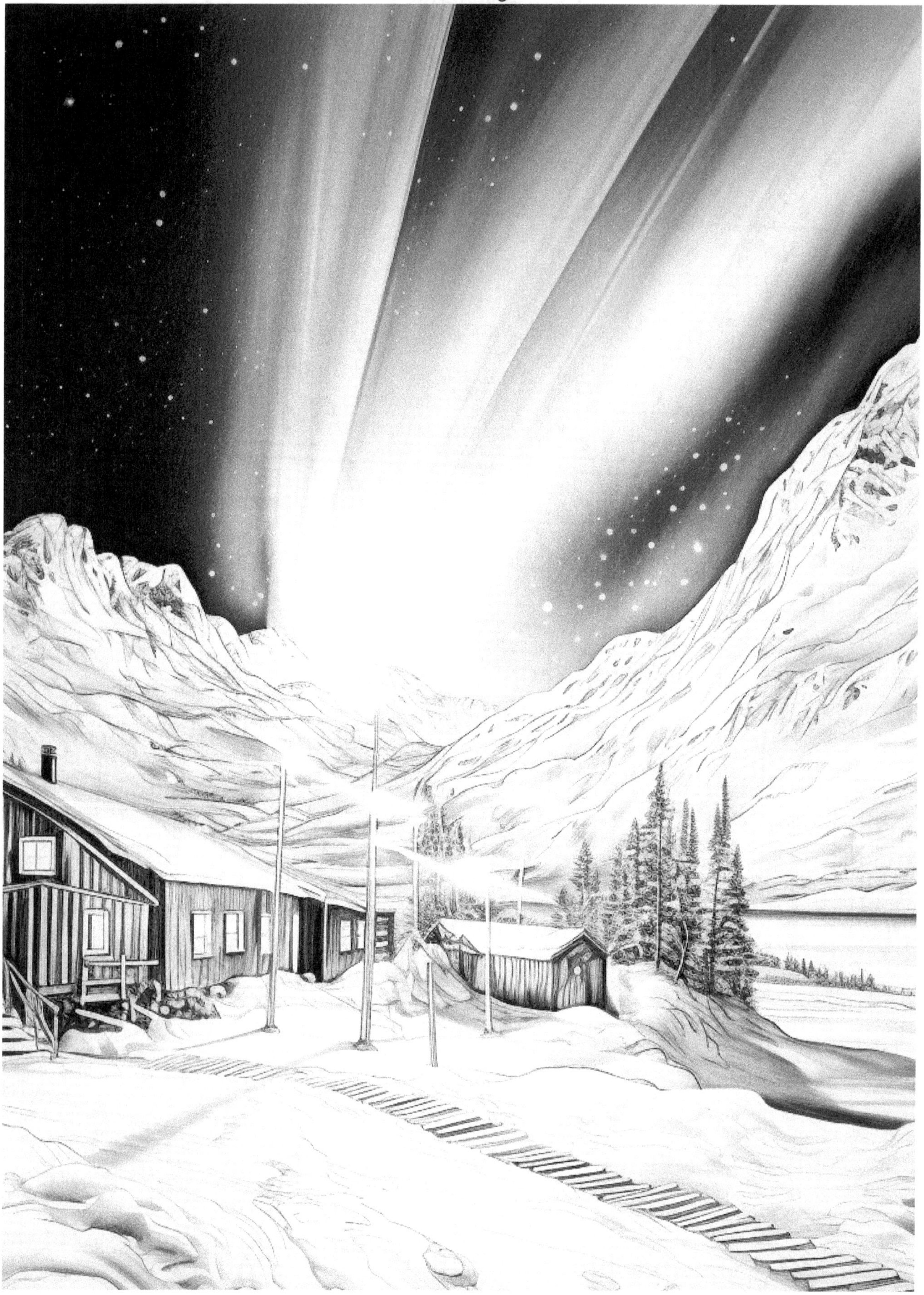

Sydney Opera House

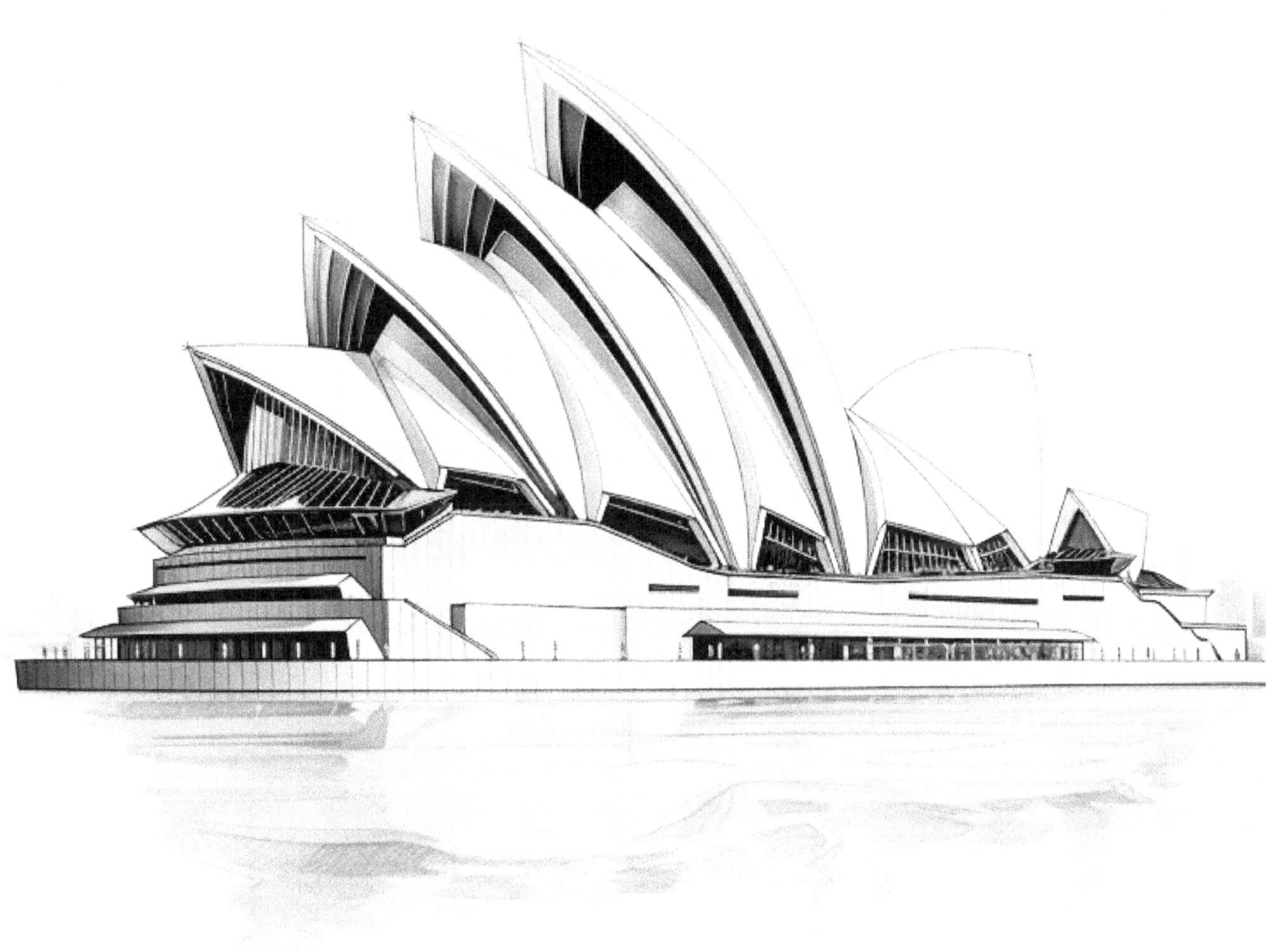

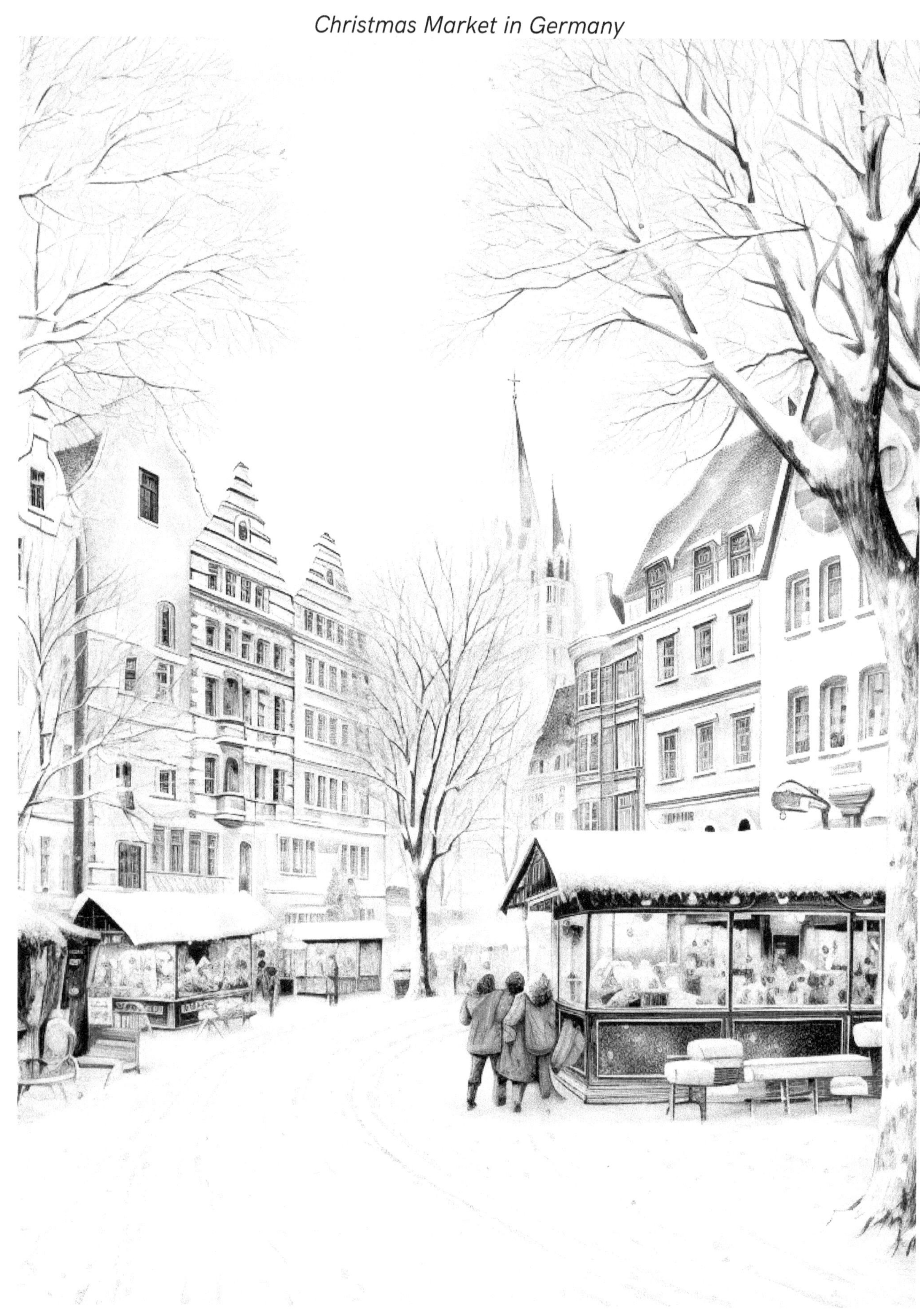

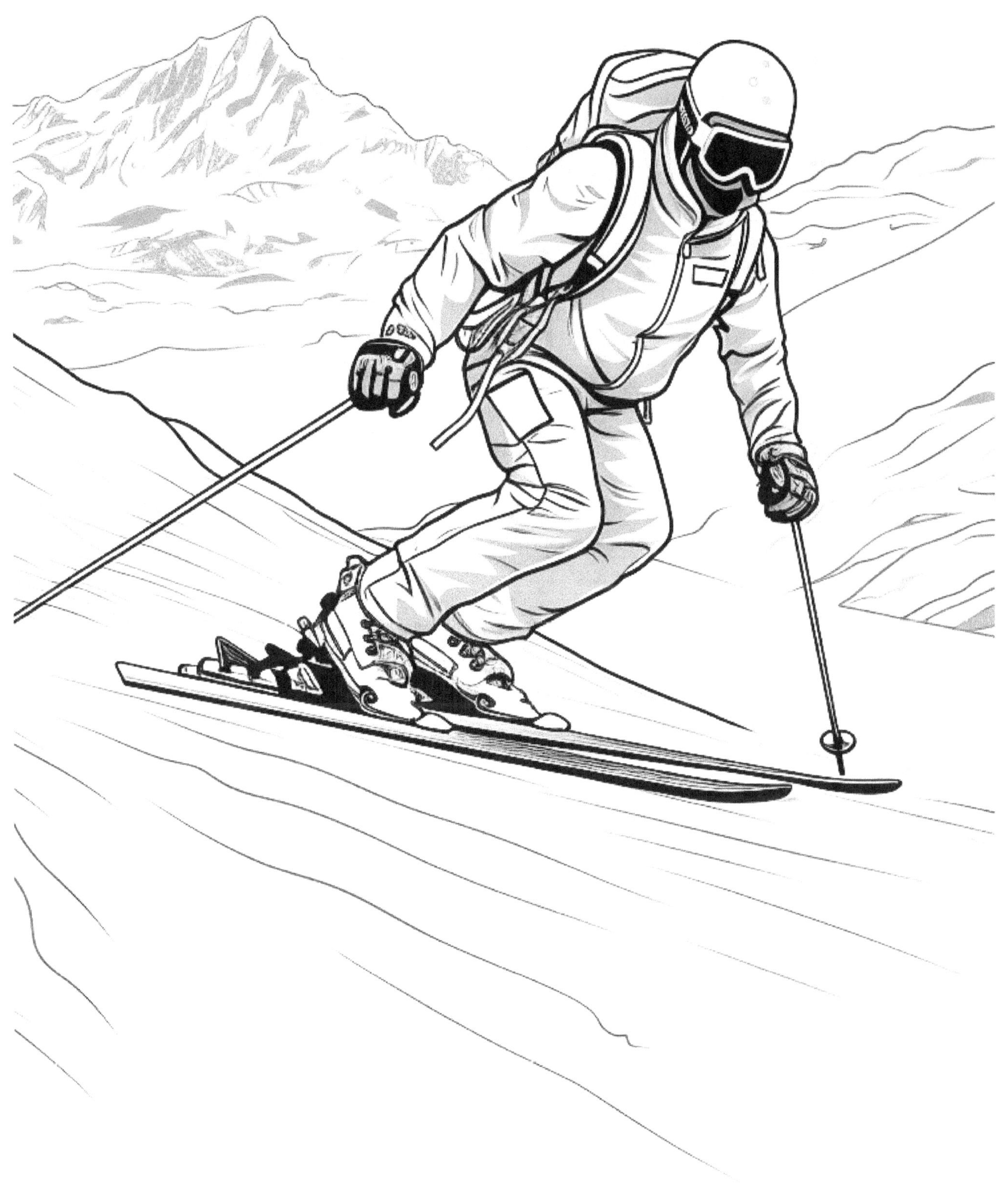

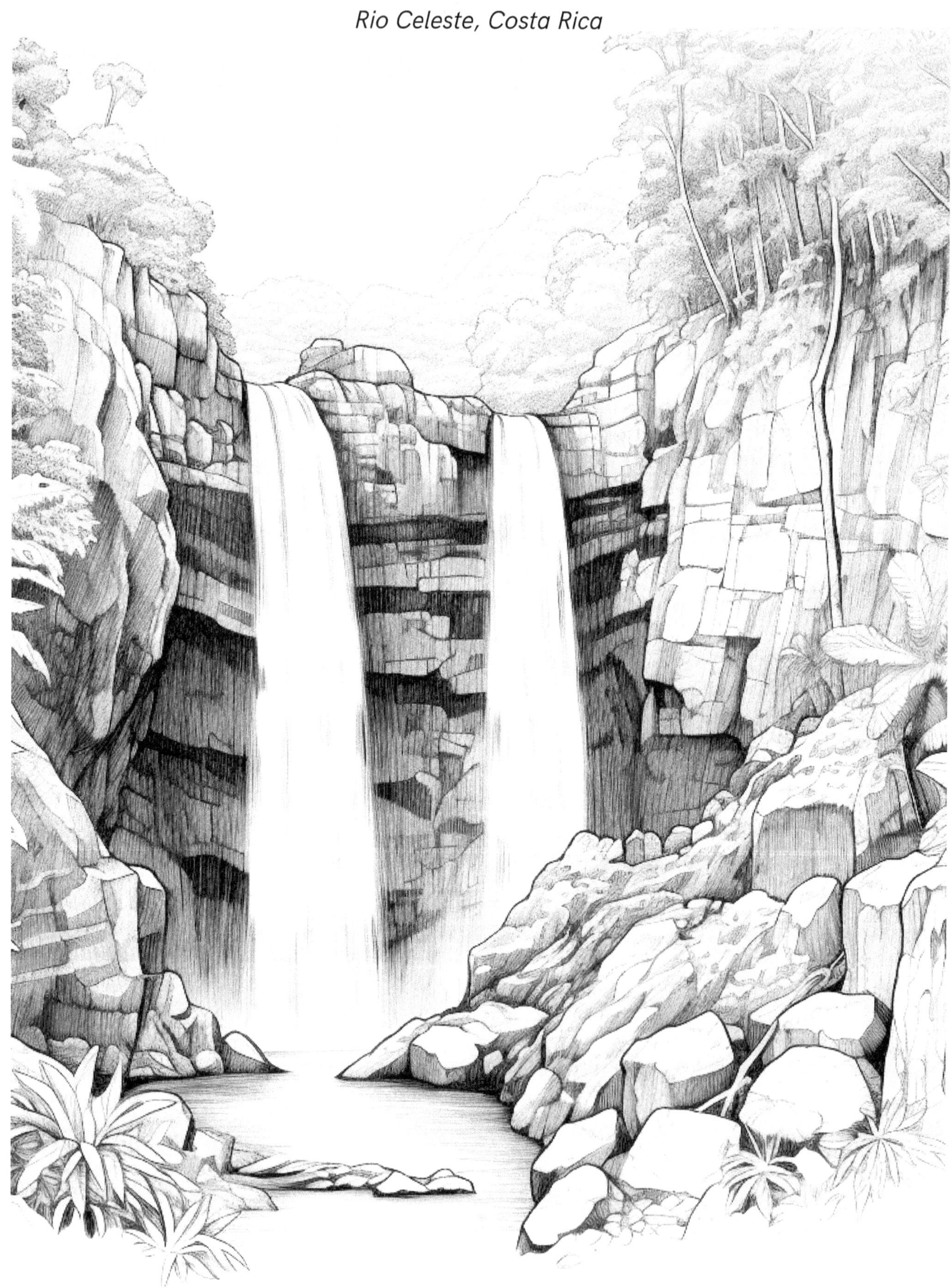

Rio Celeste, Costa Rica

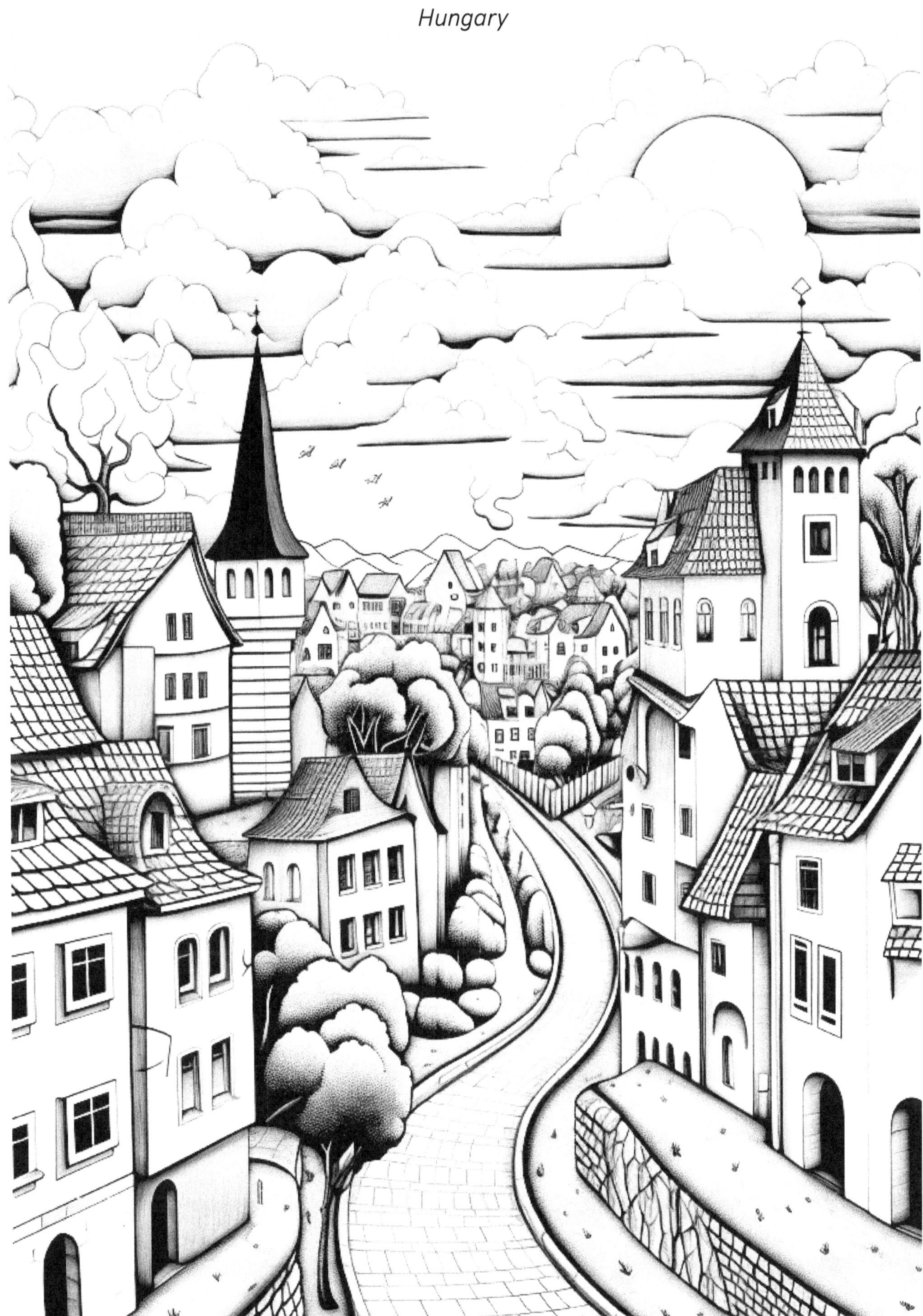
Hungary

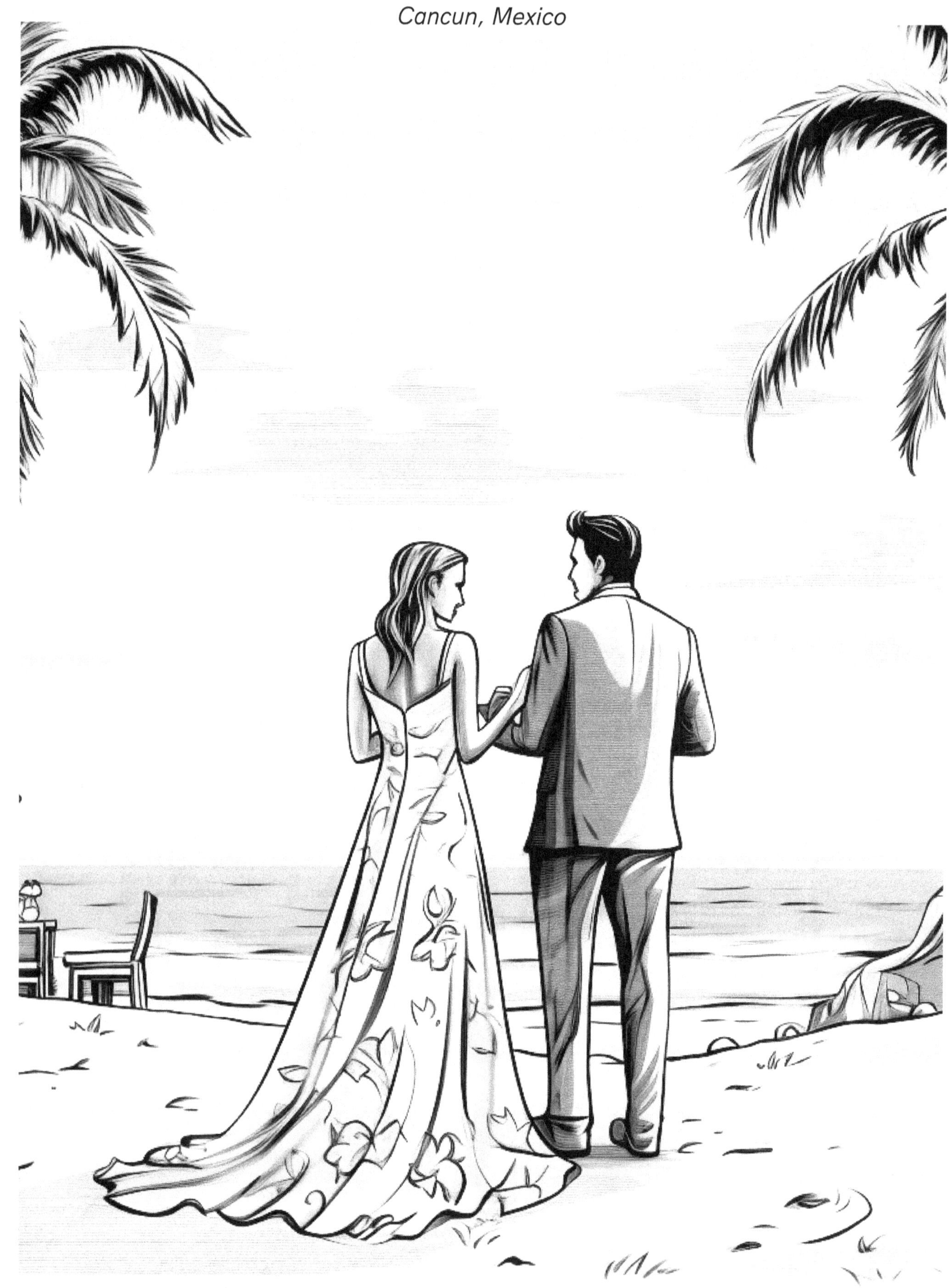

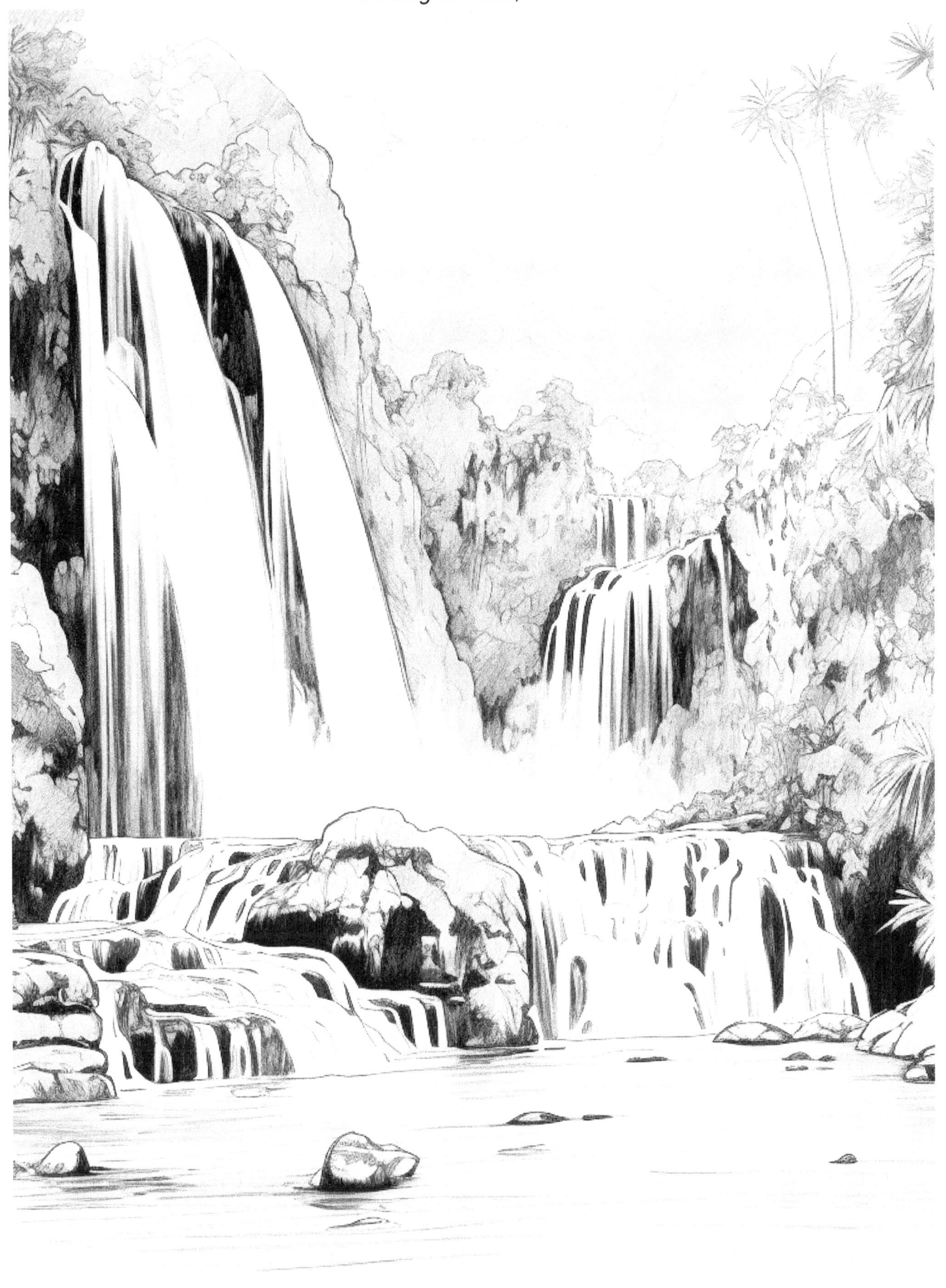

Khang Si Falls, Laos

Lake Como, Italy

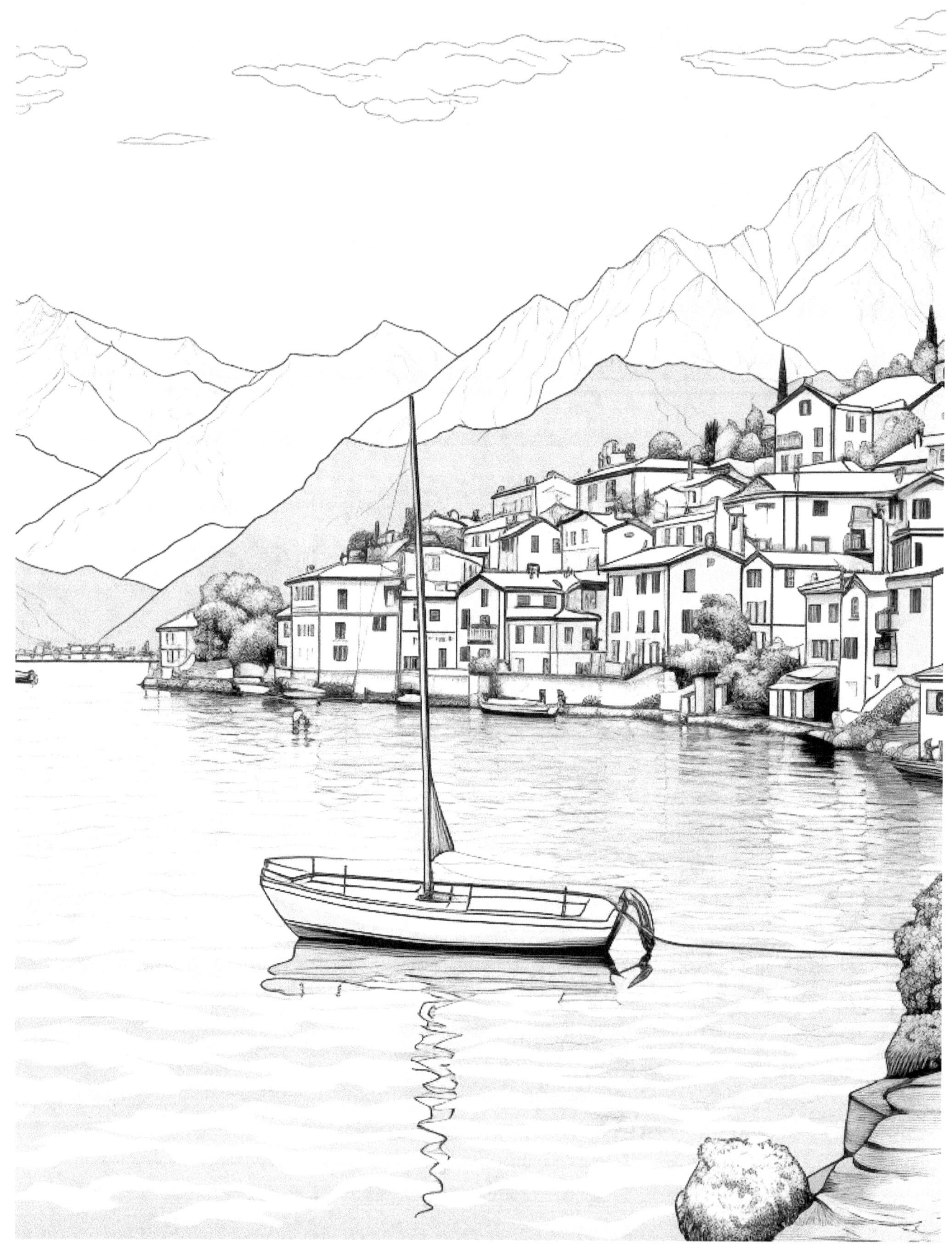

Lapland, Finland

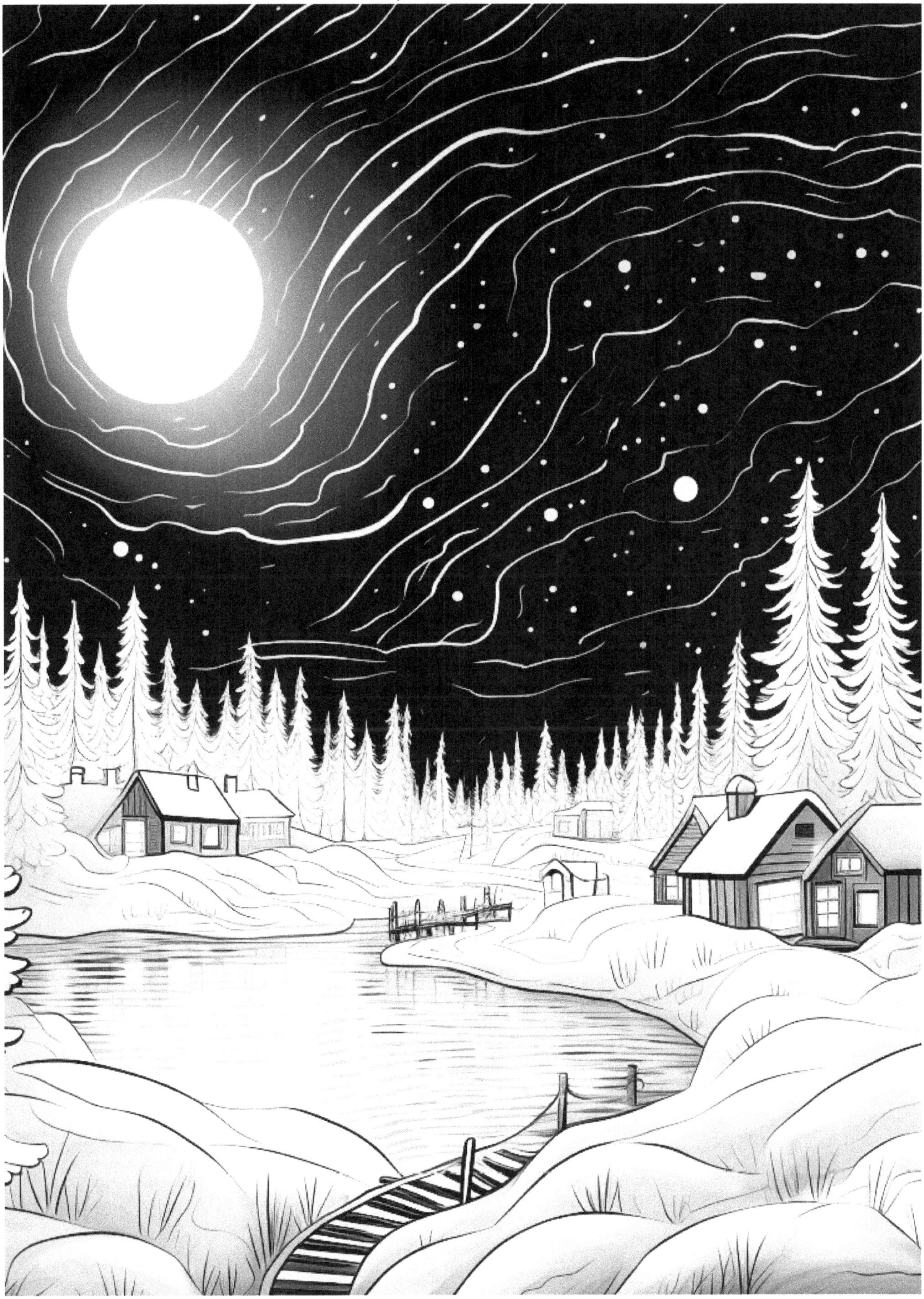

The Pitons, St. Lucia

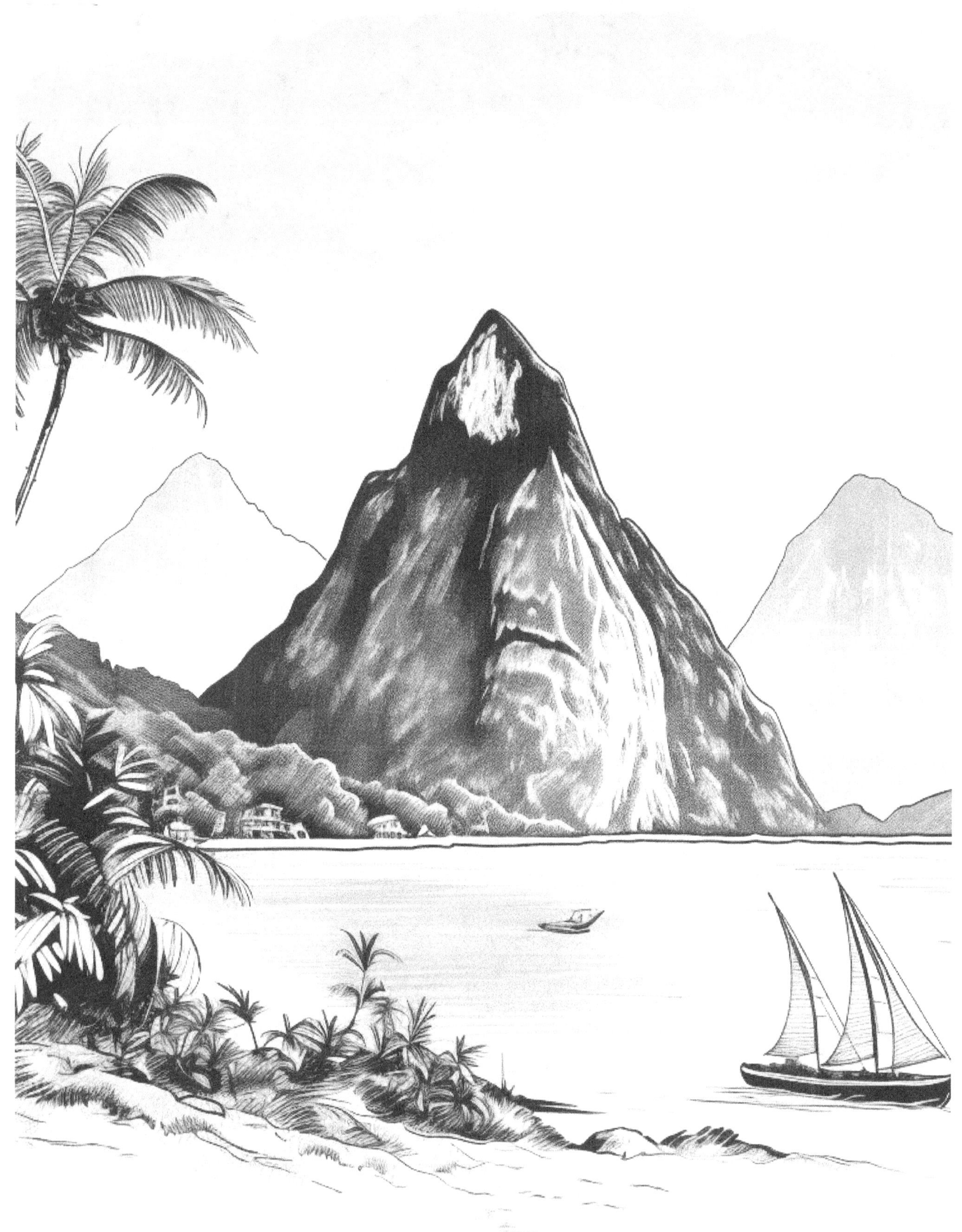

Vietnamese Fisherman

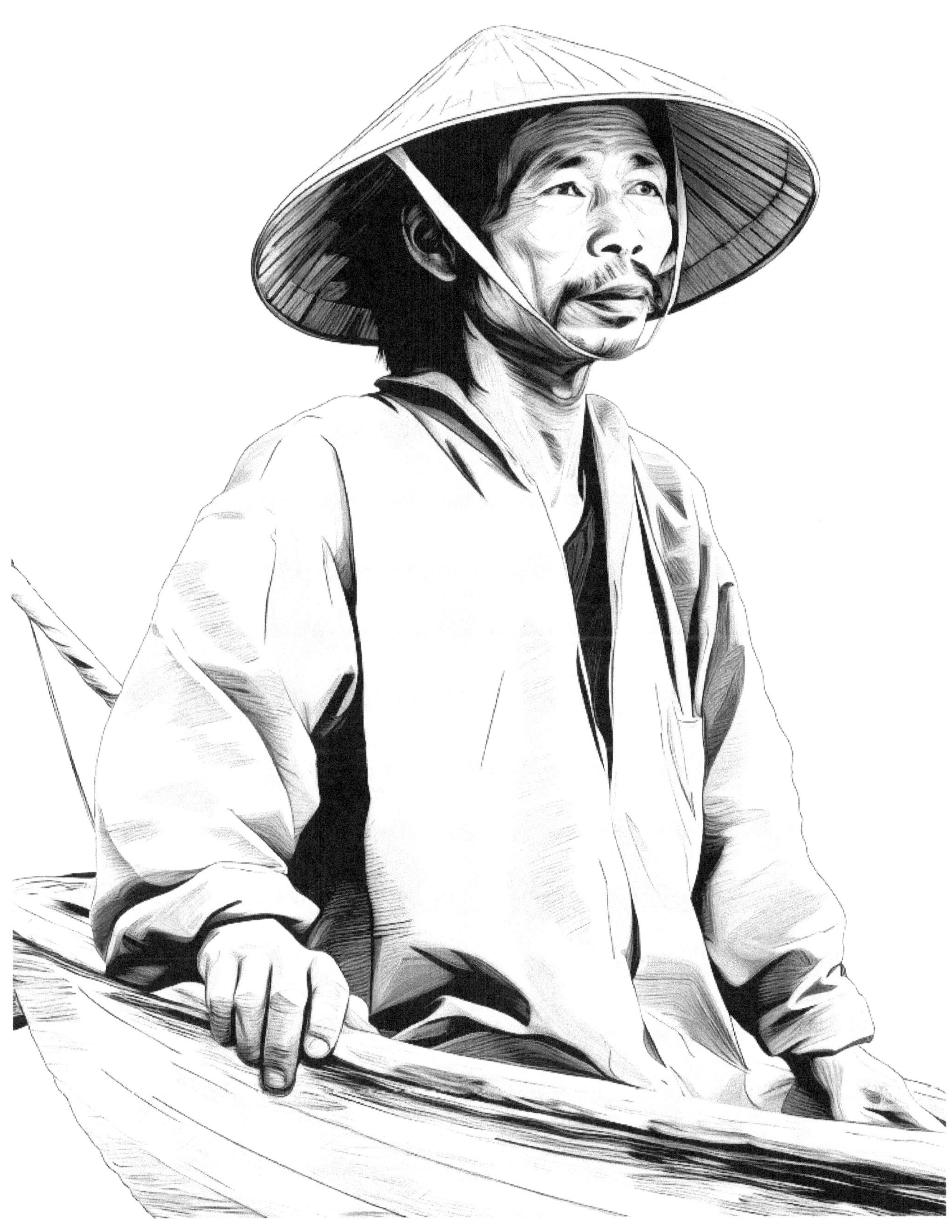

The Netherlands

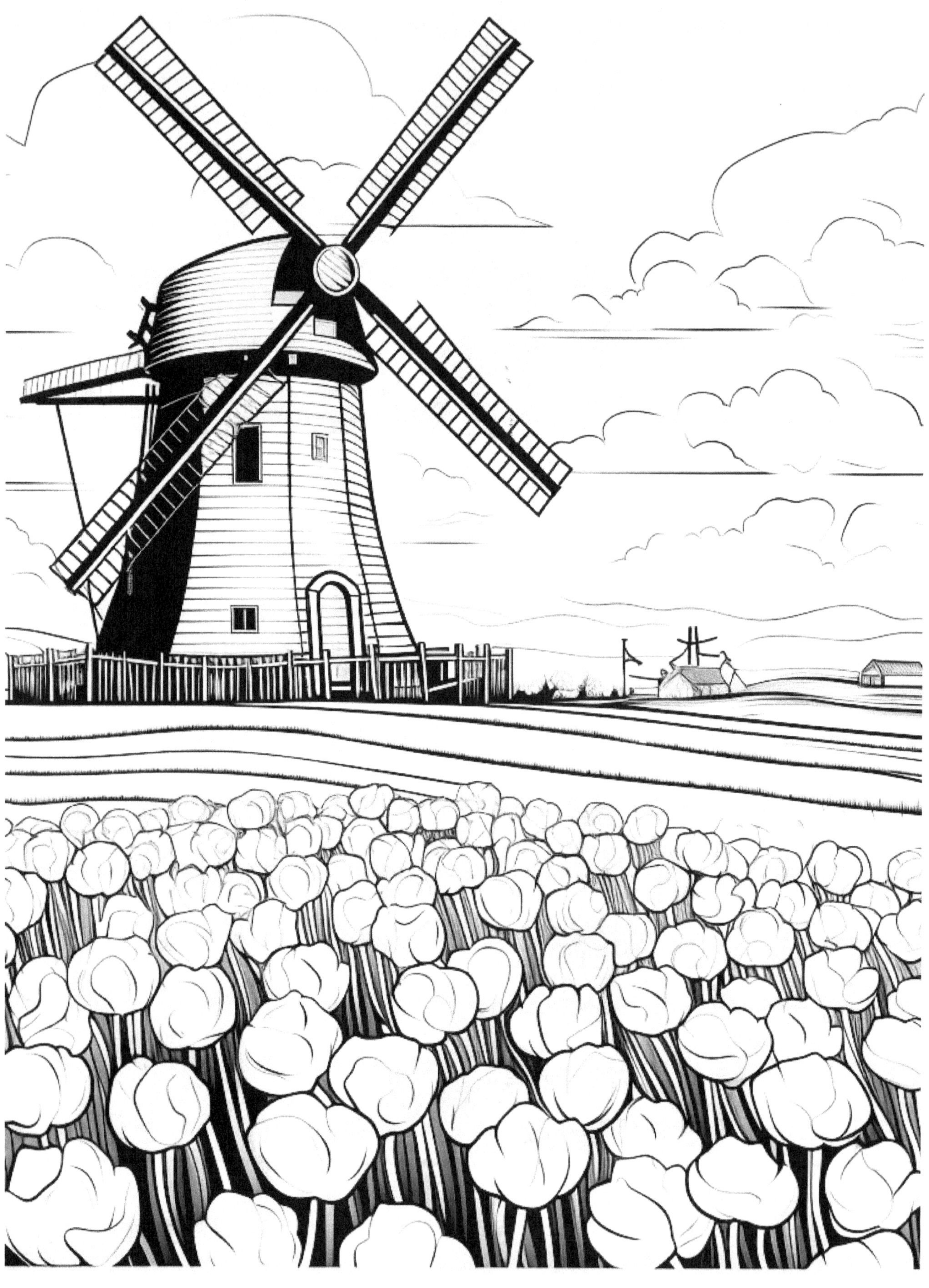

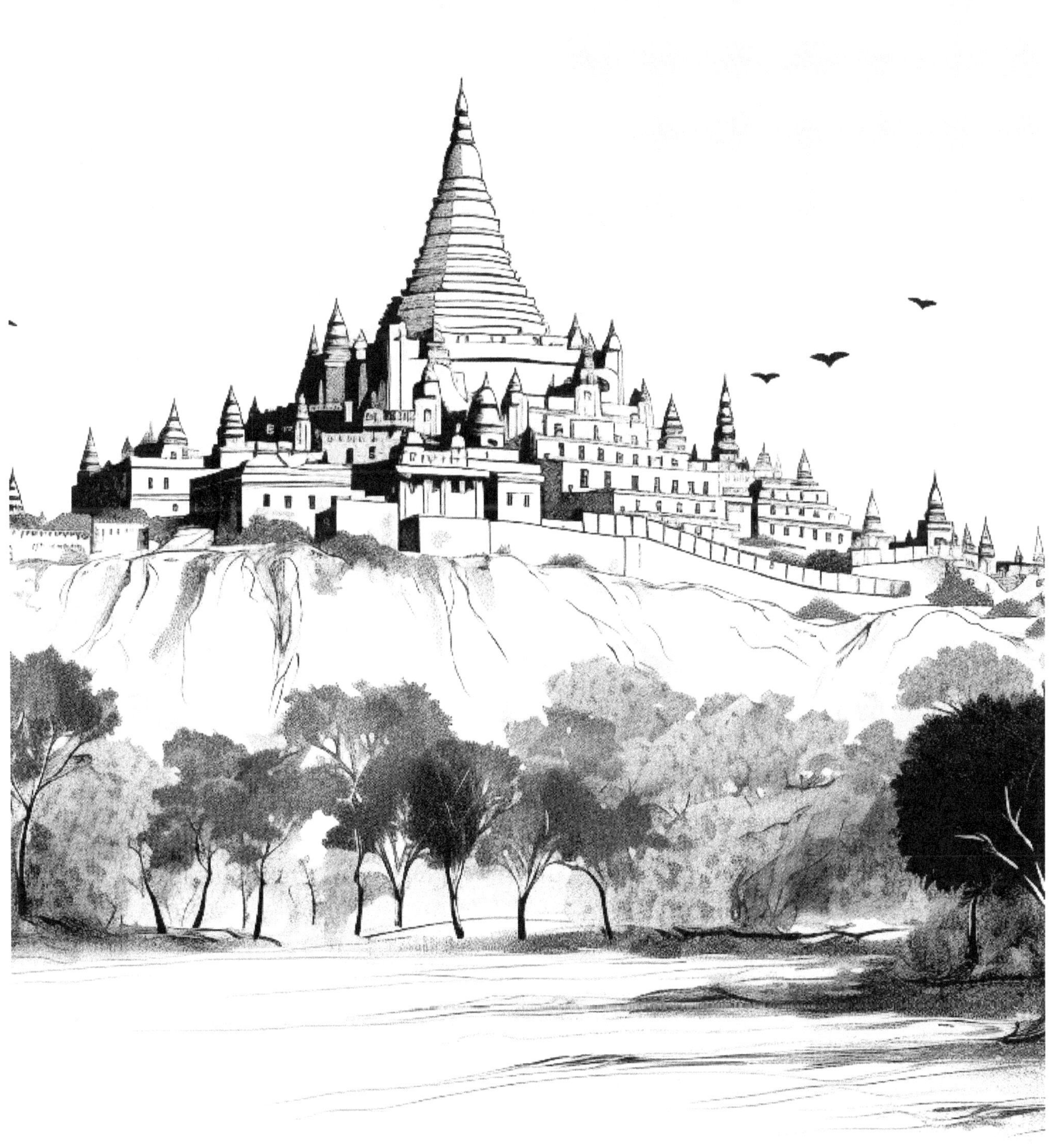

Bagan, Myanmar

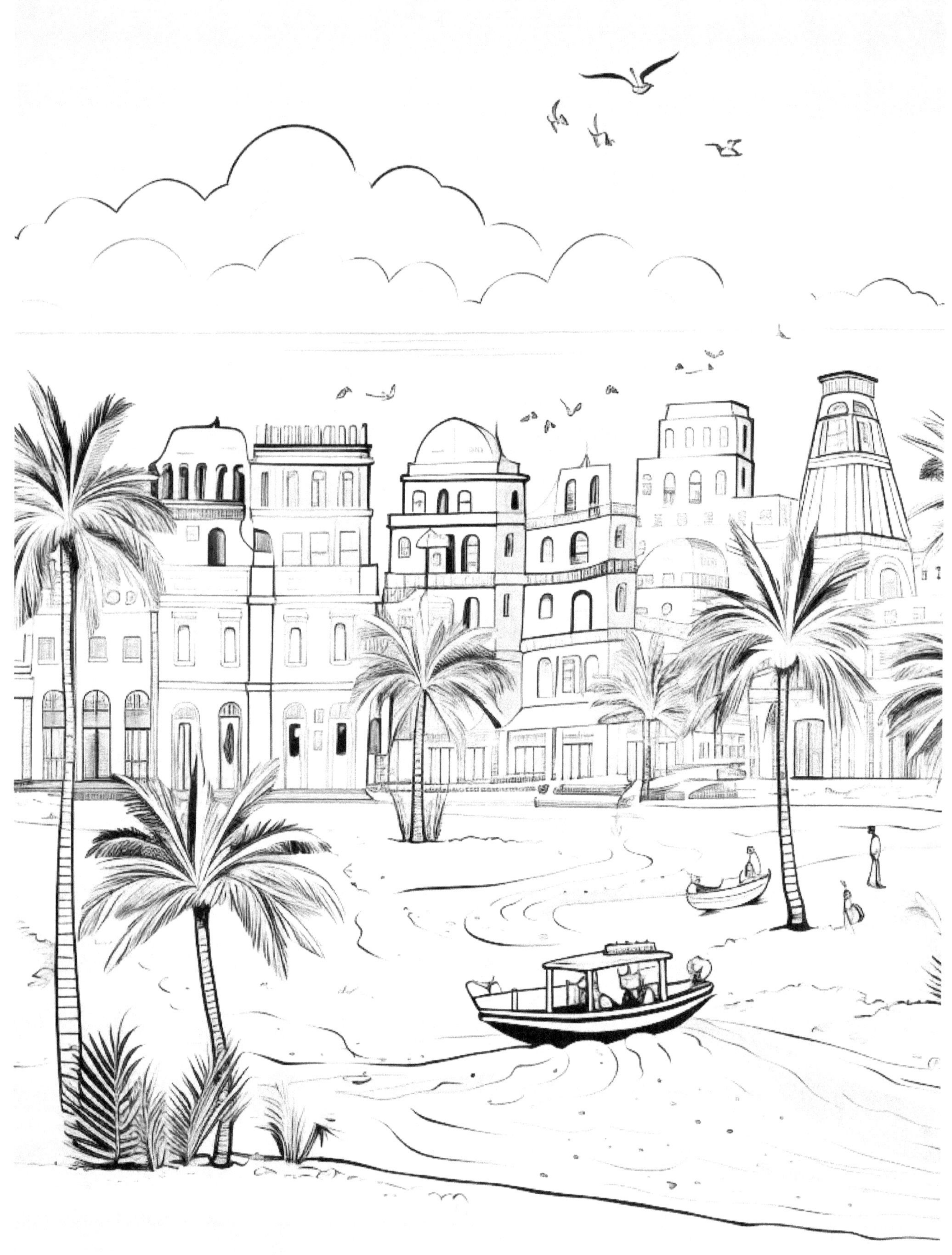

Chamarel, Mauritius

Hallstatt, Austria

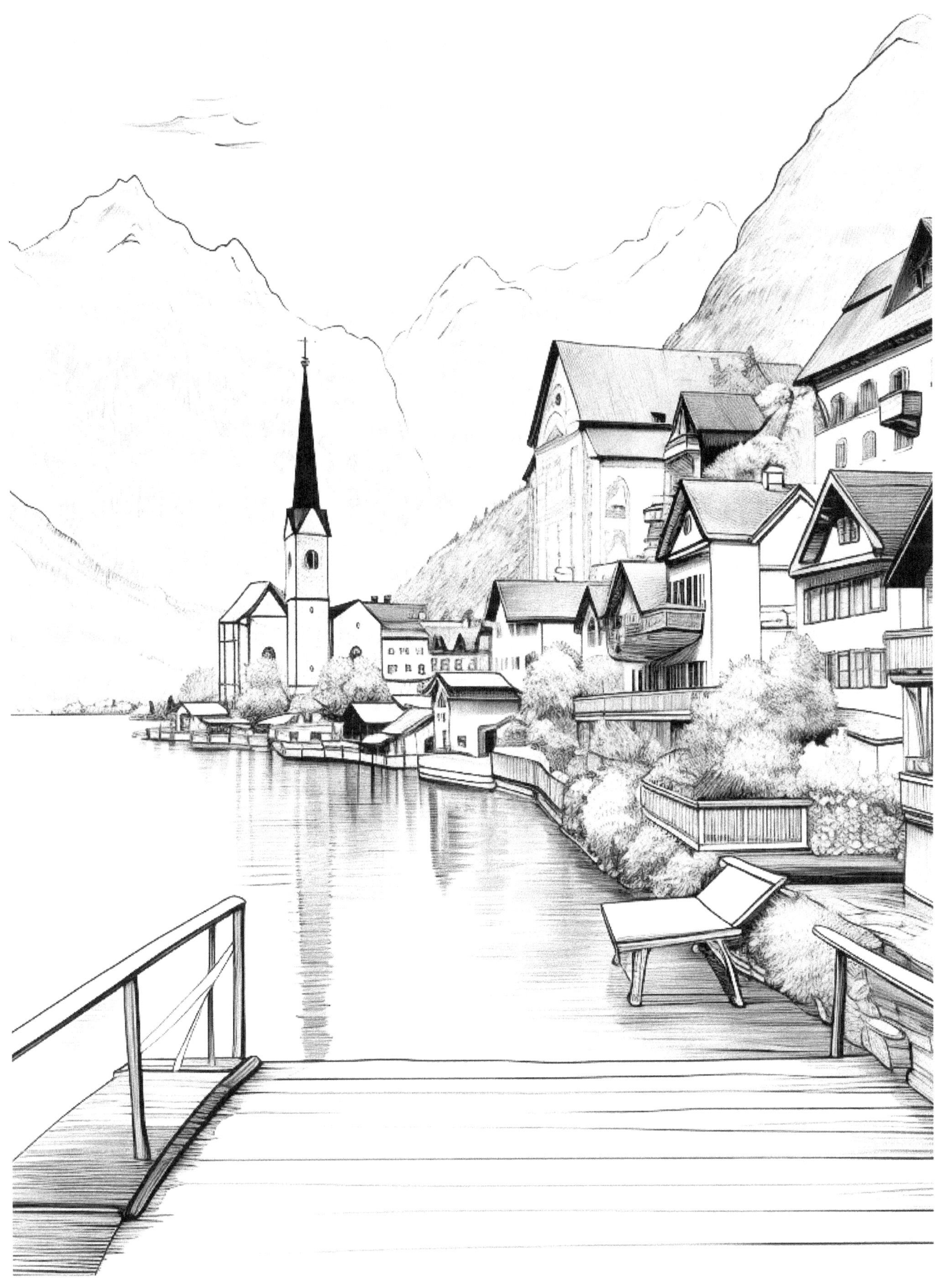

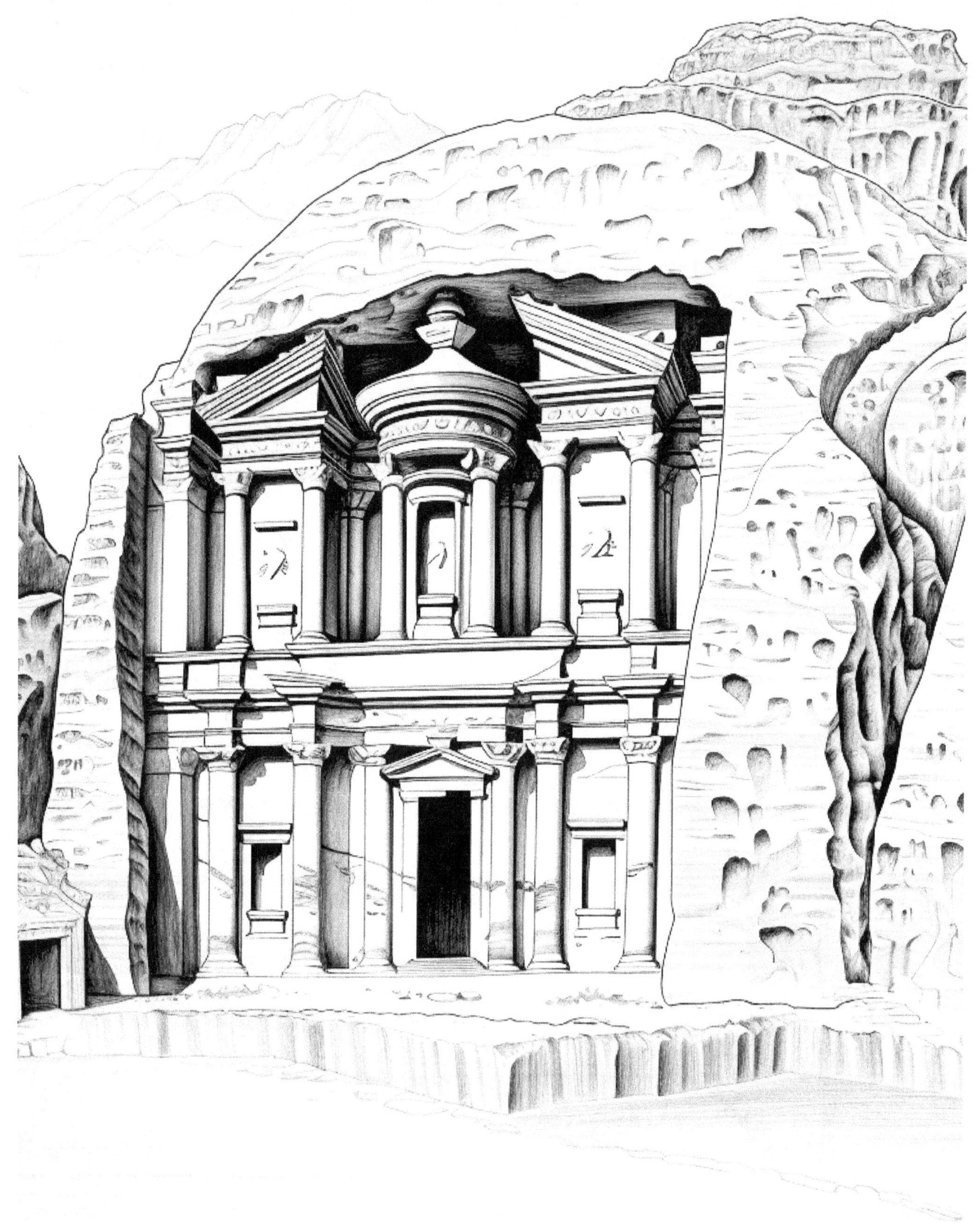

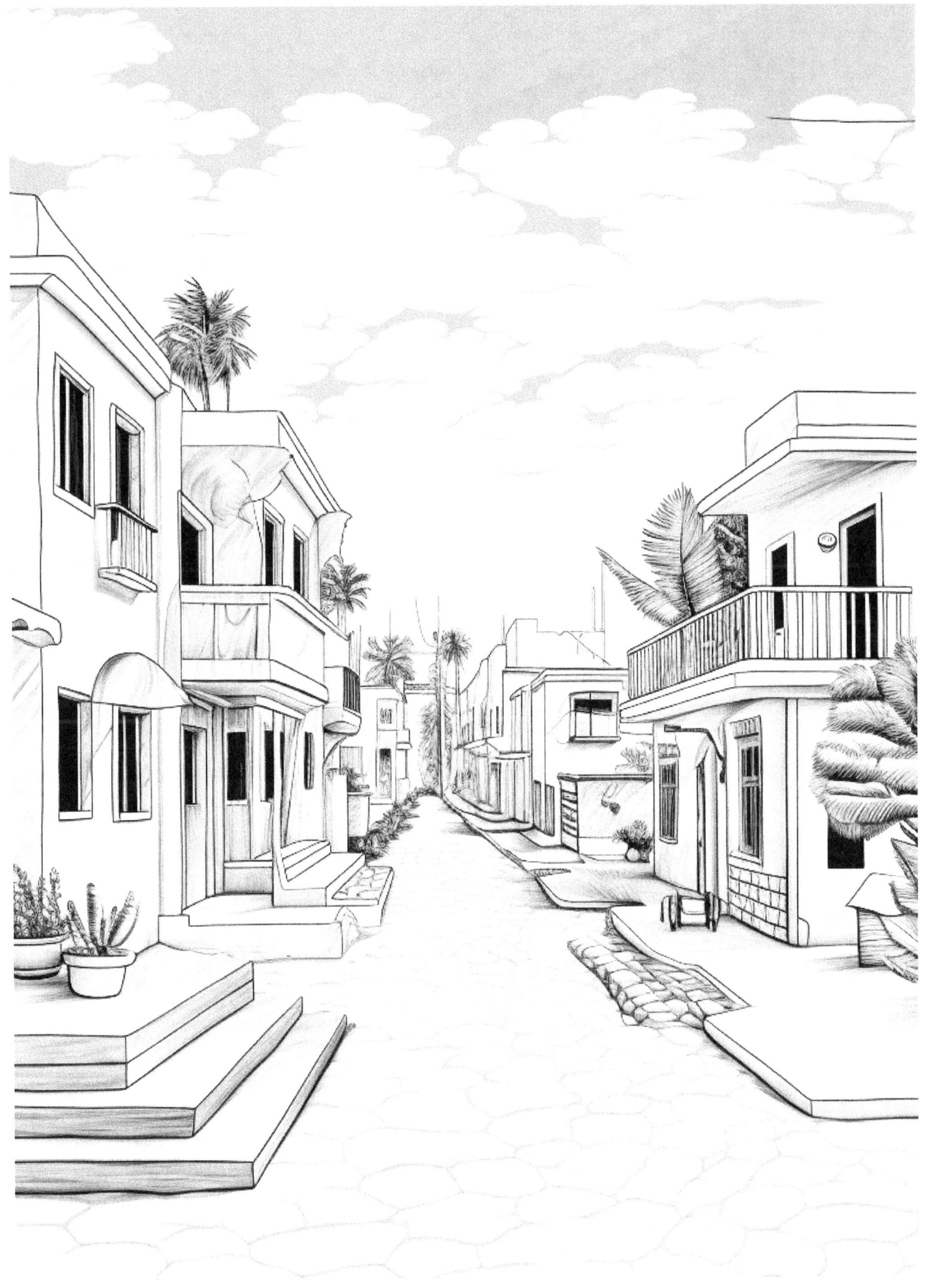

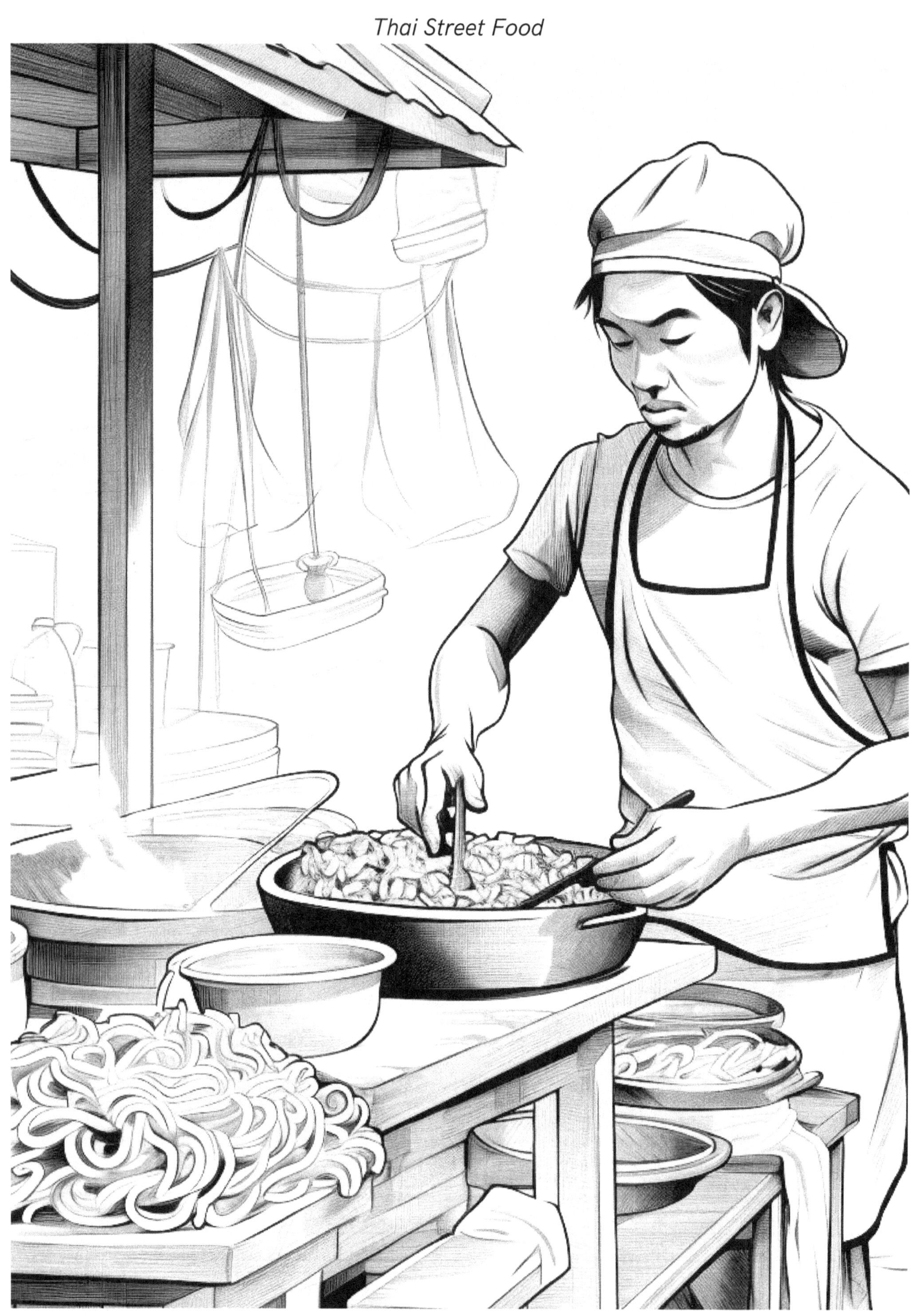

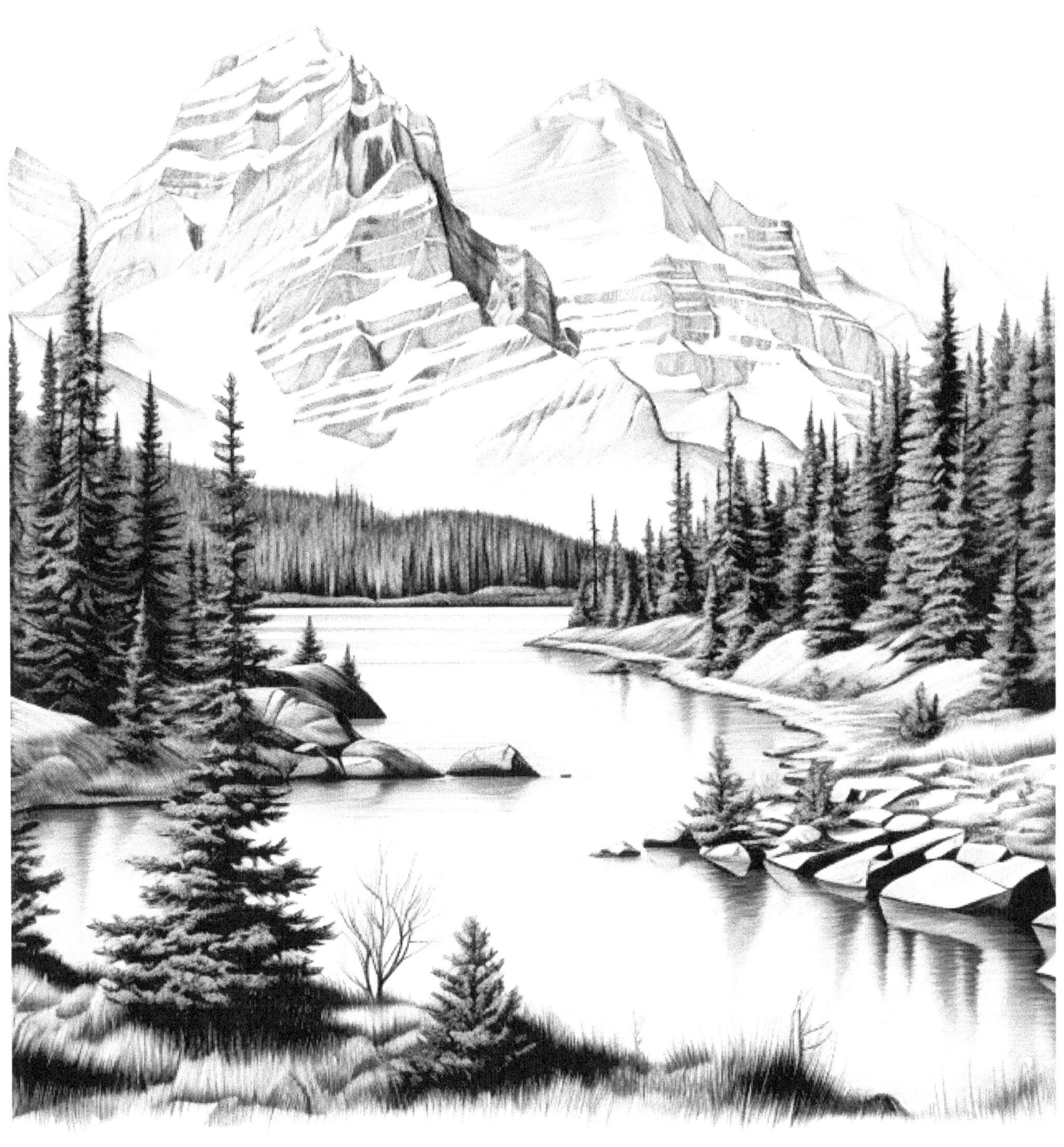

Banff National Park, Canada

Hawa Mahal, India

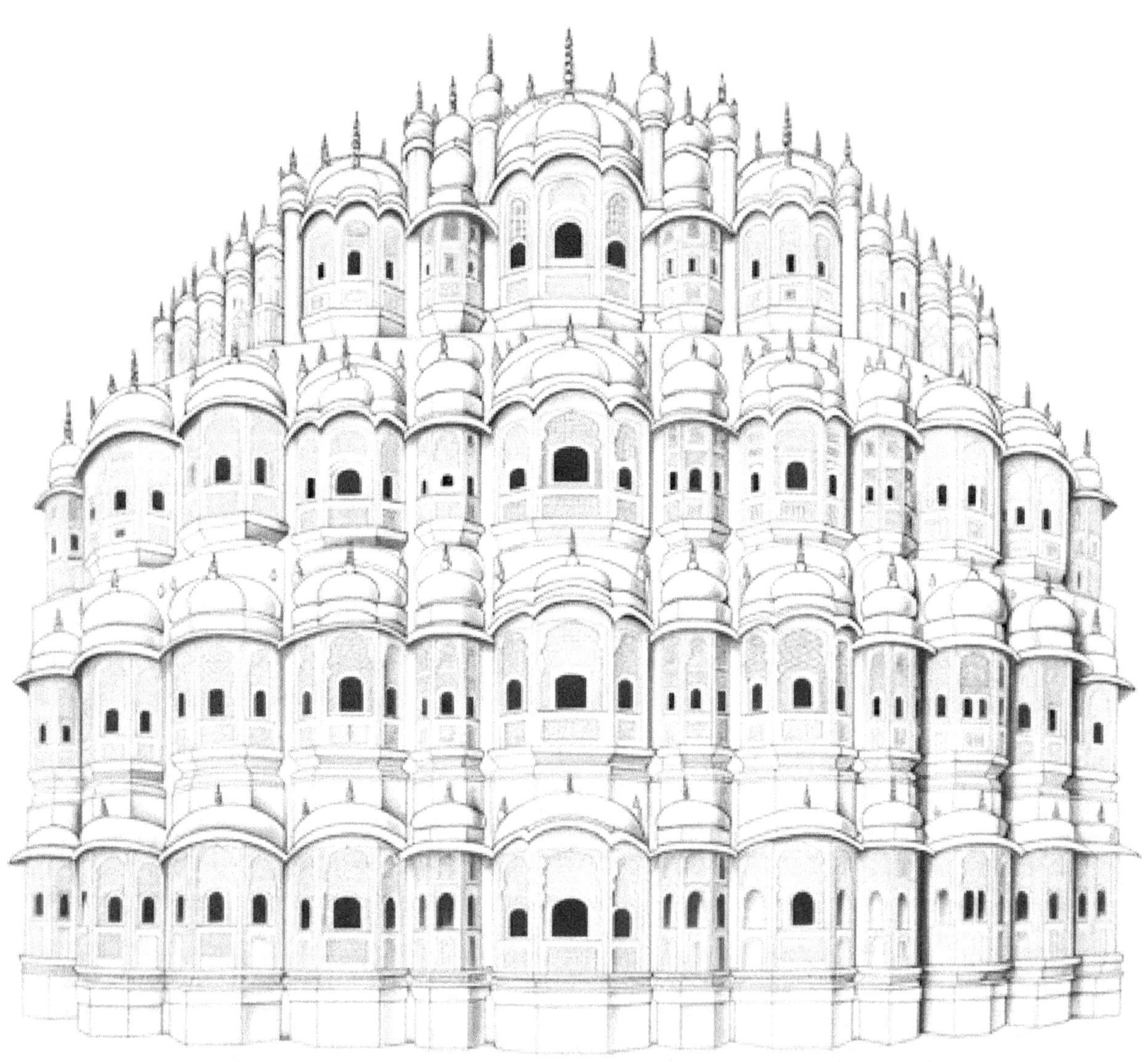

Seychelles

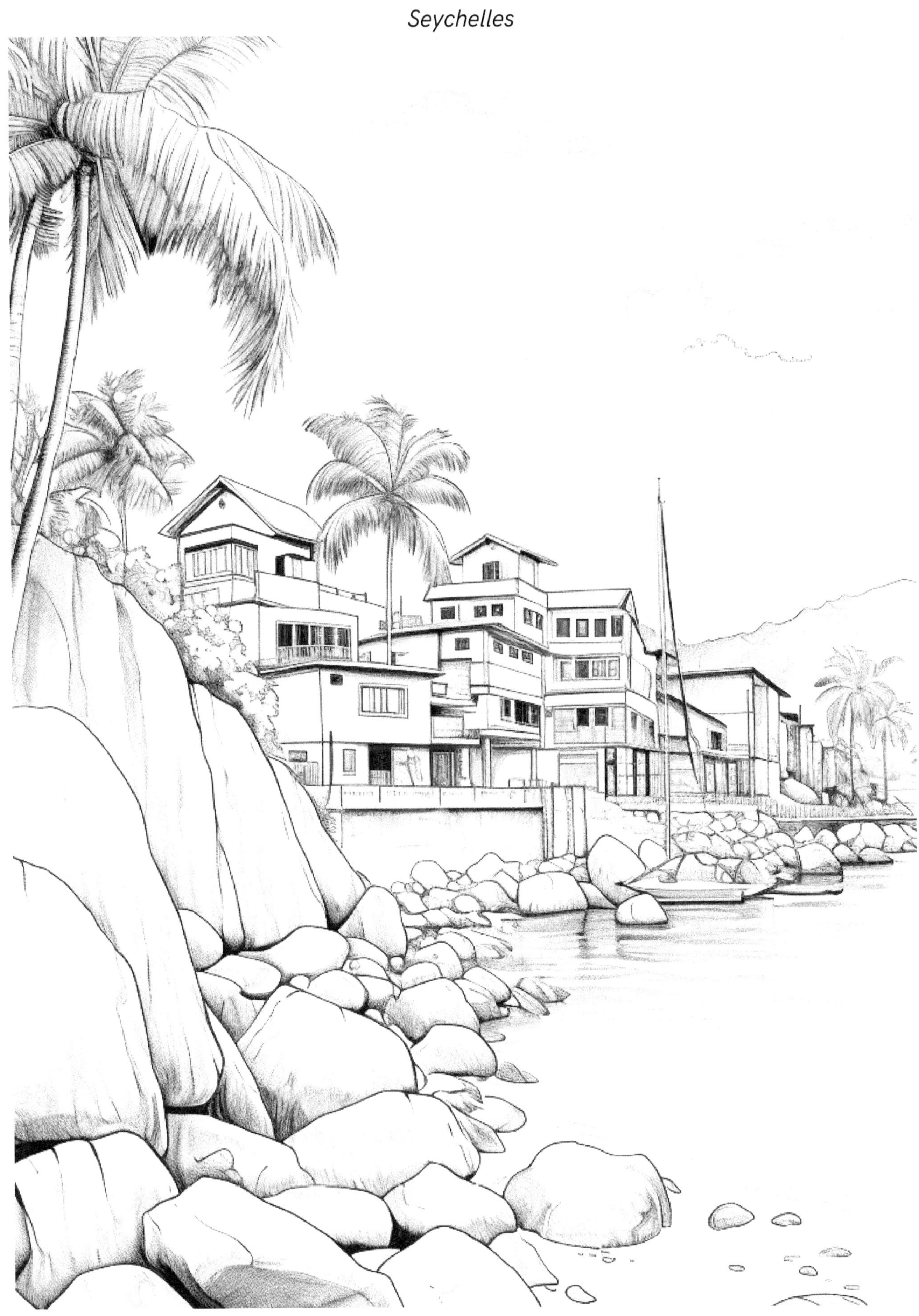

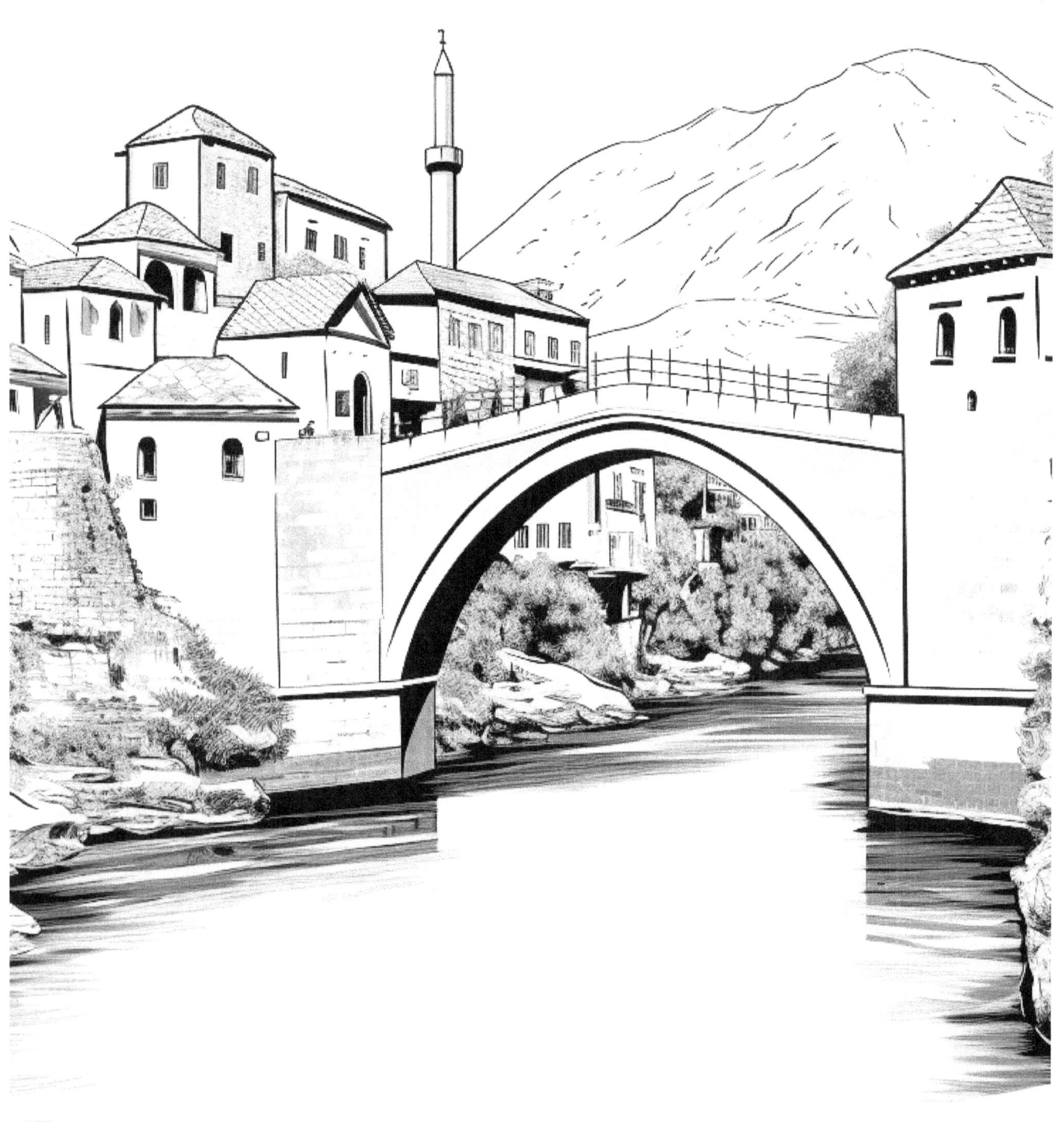

Mostar, Bosnia

Alaska, USA

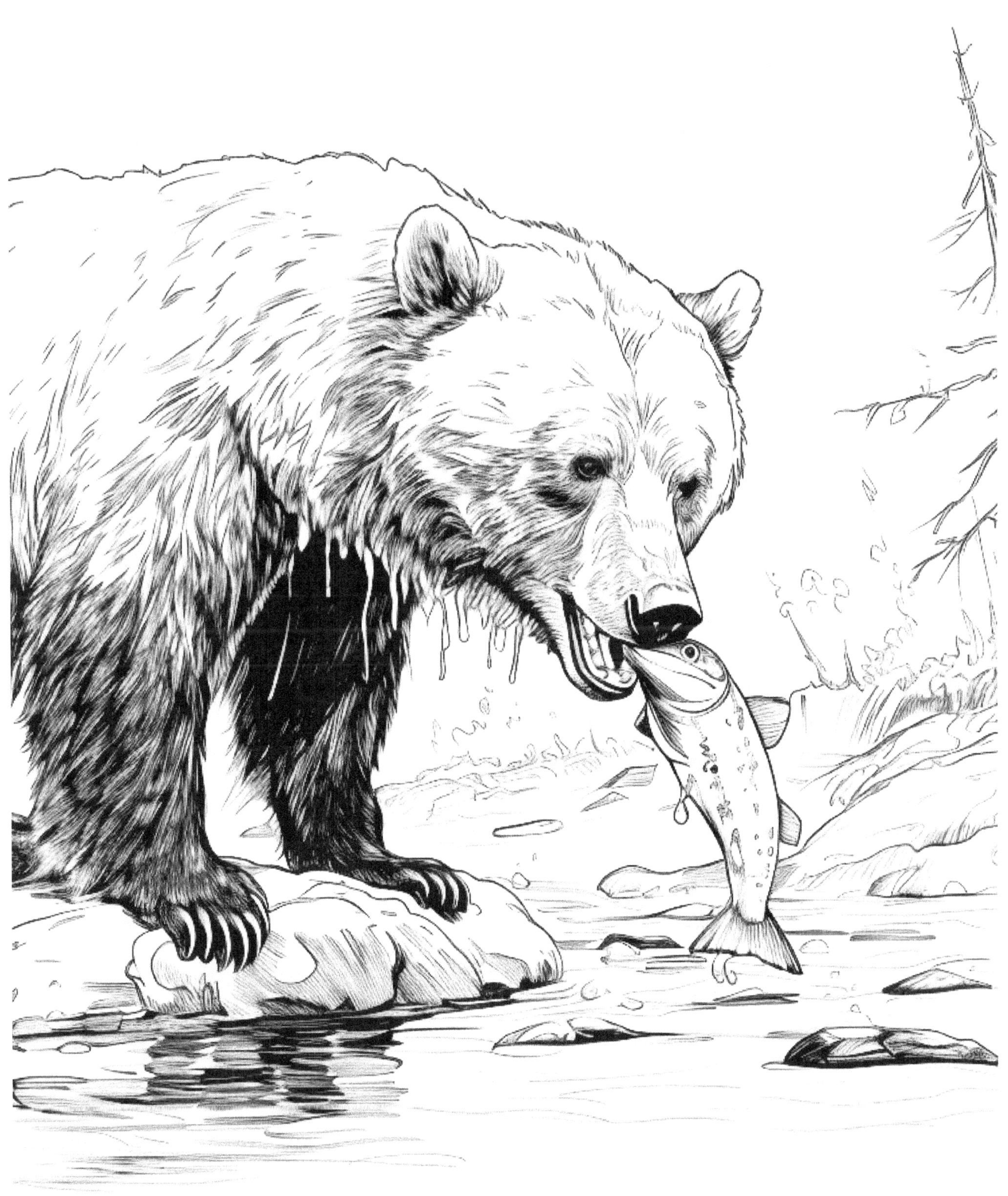

Monaco

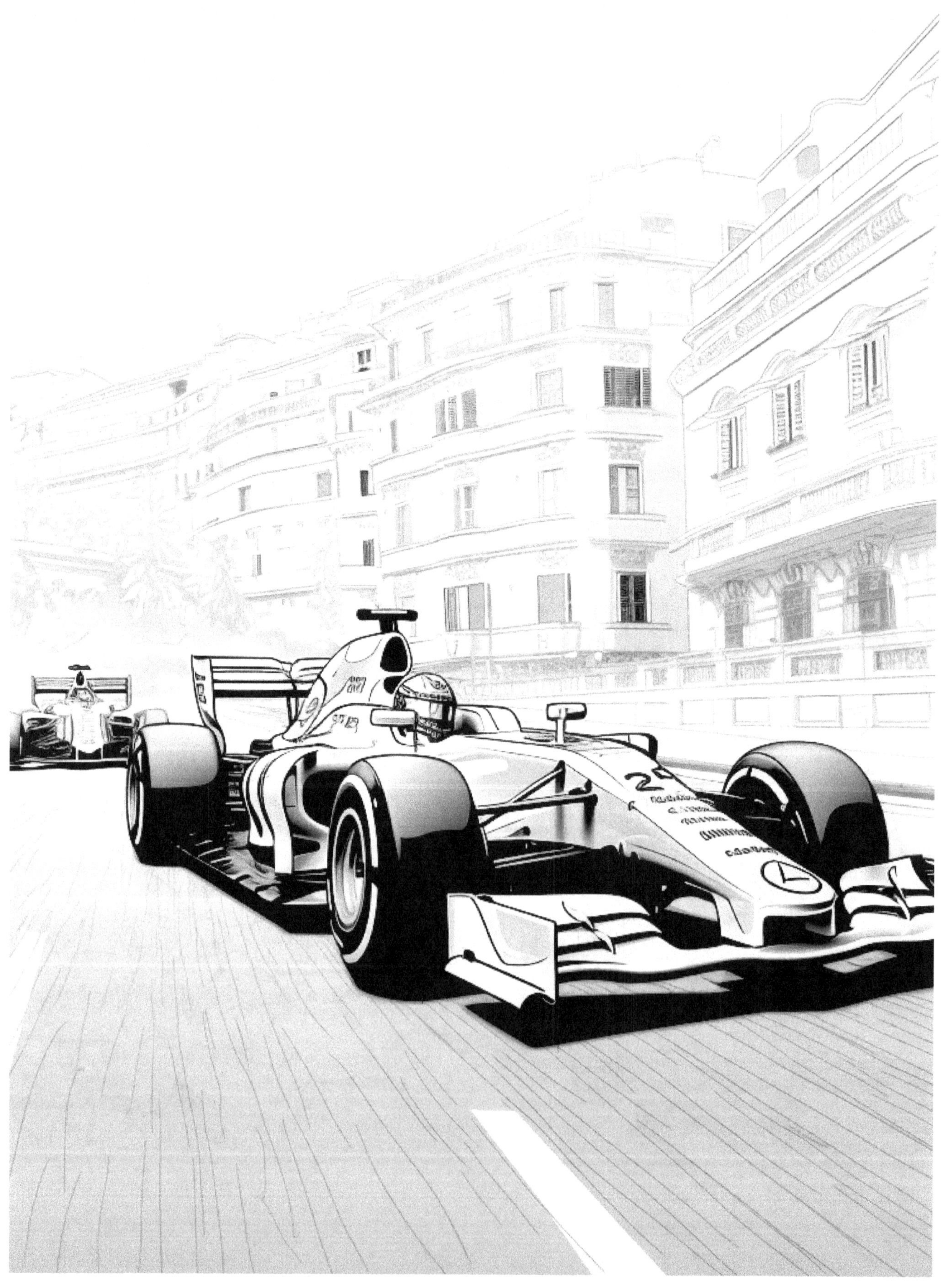

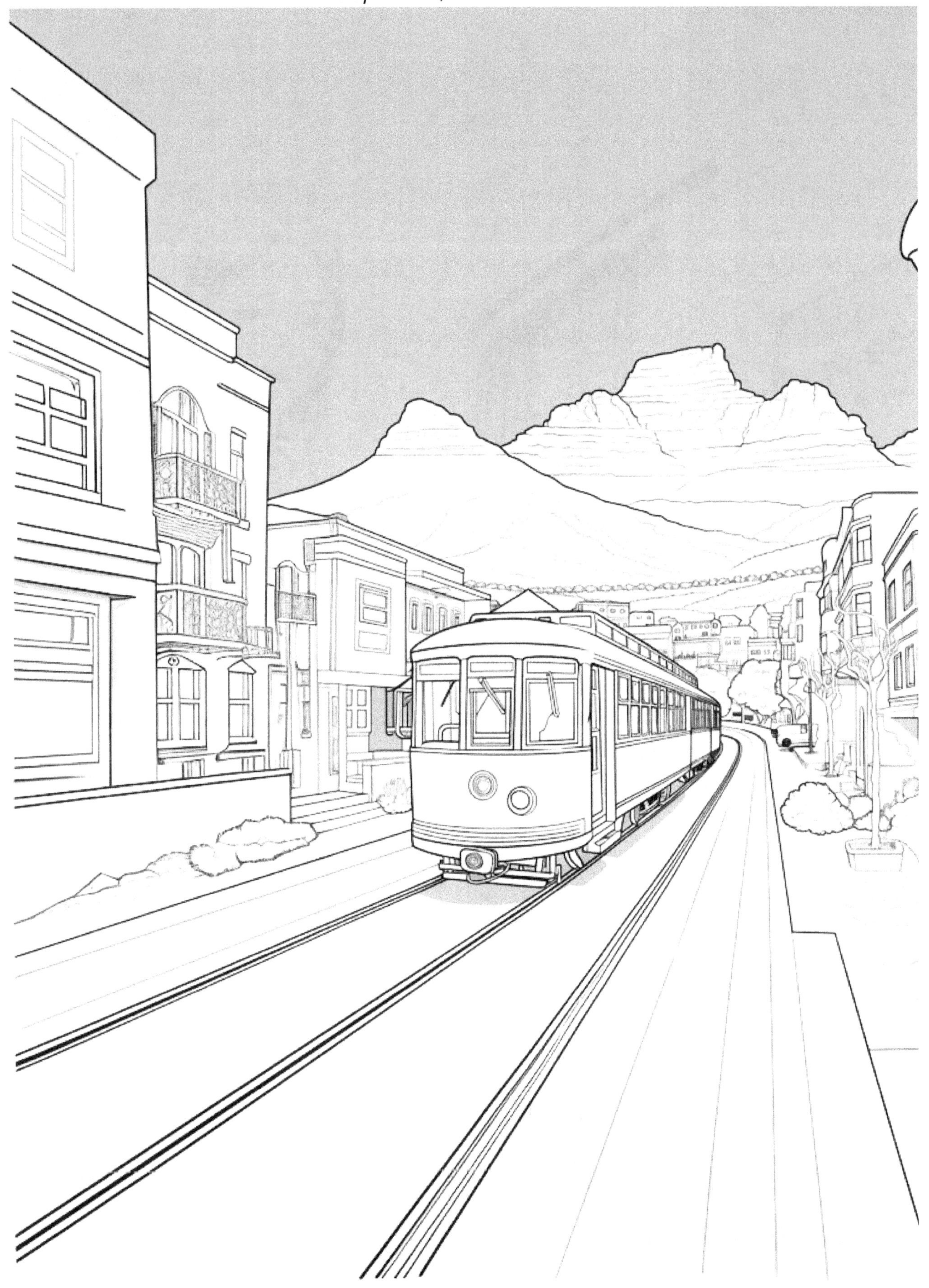

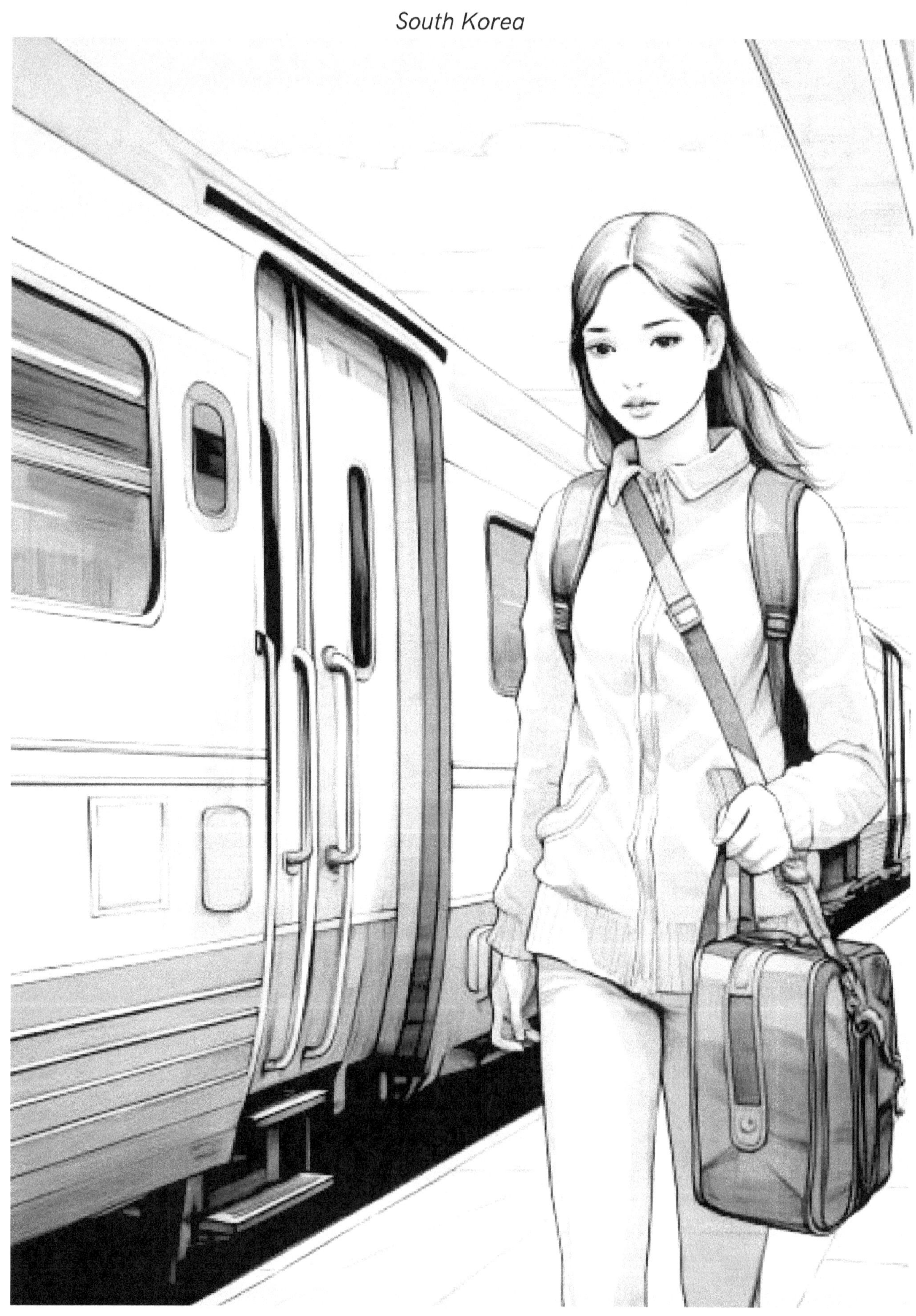

South Korea

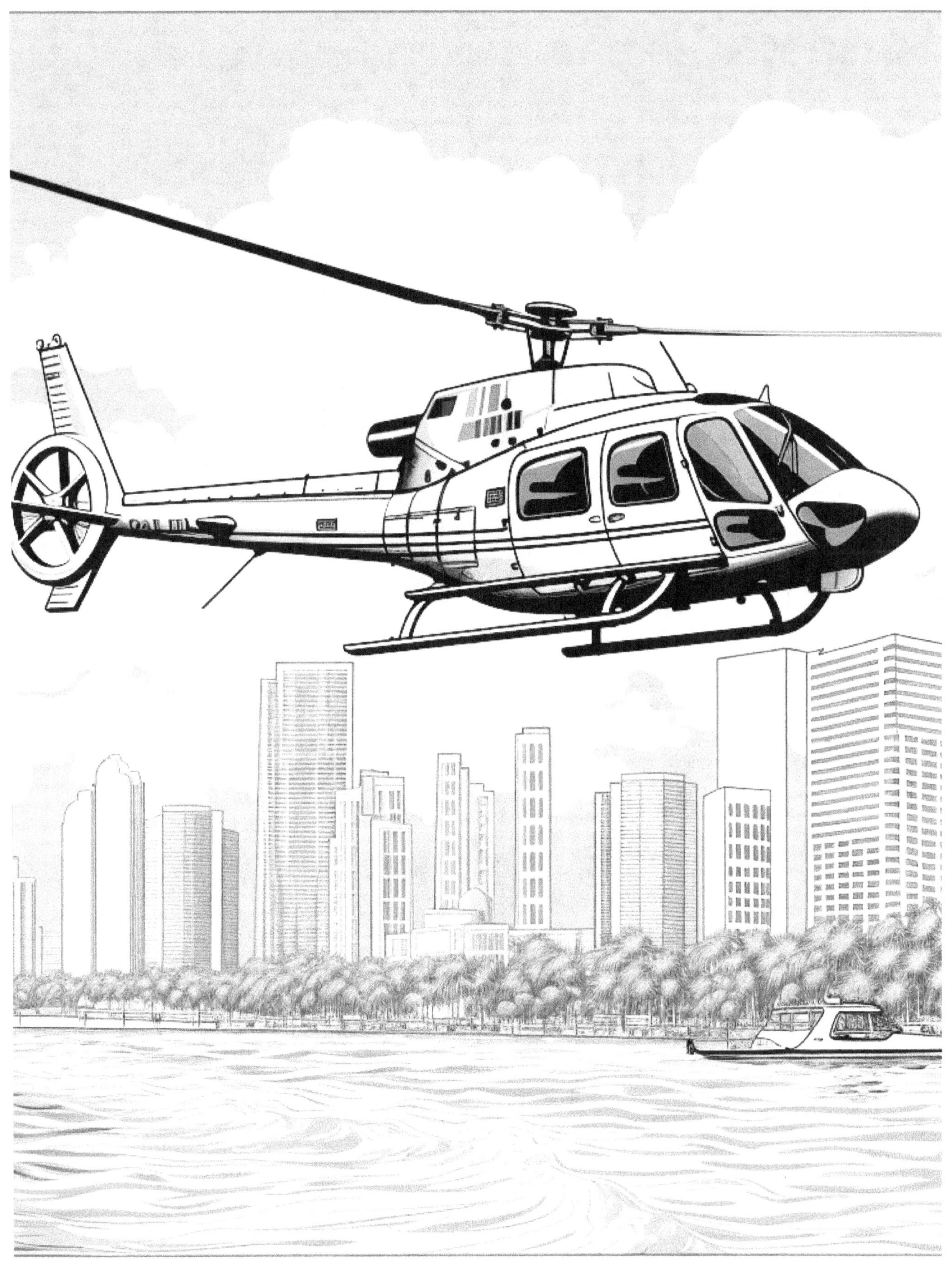

The Great Migration of the Wilderbeast in Africa

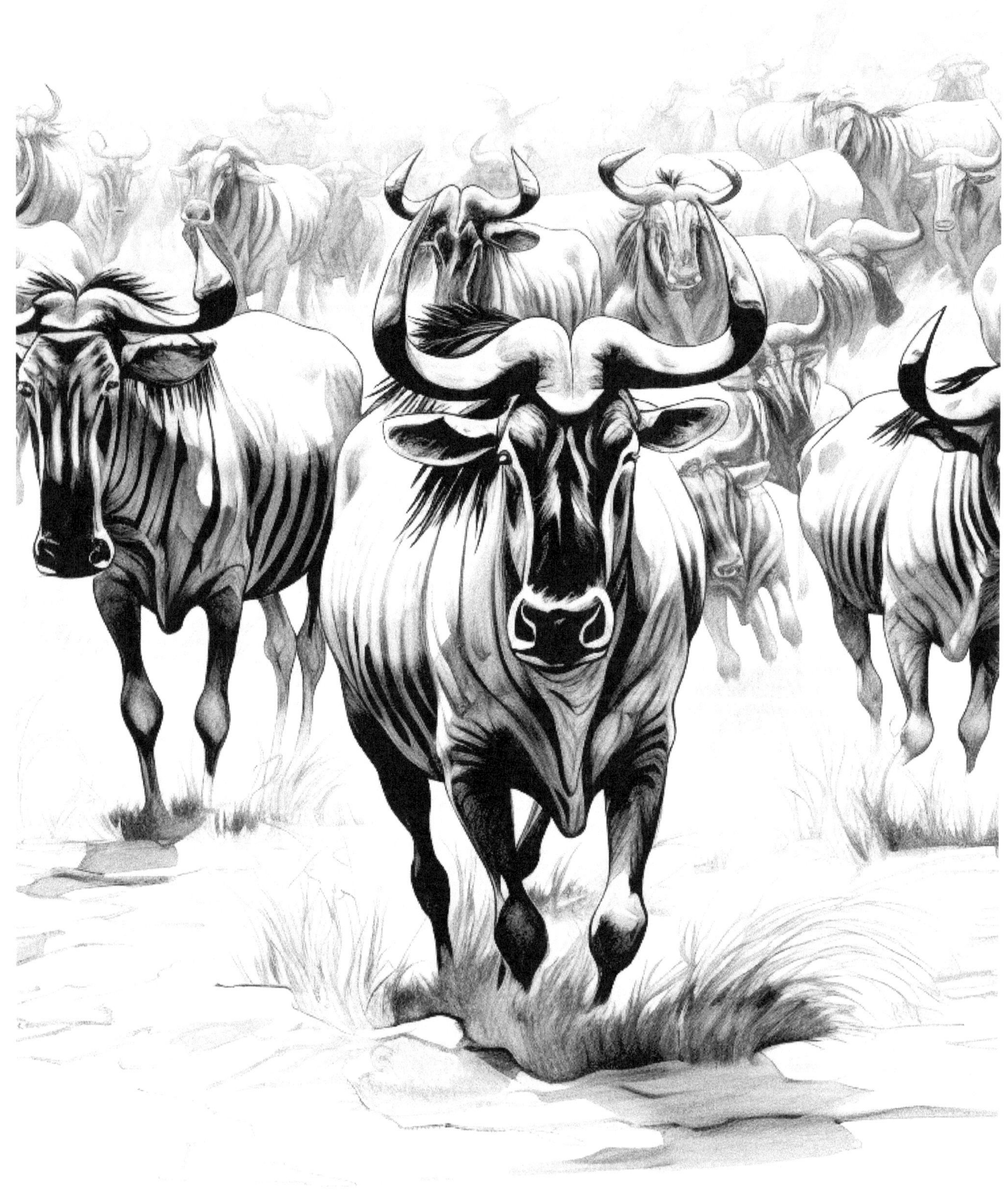

Taiwanese Boba

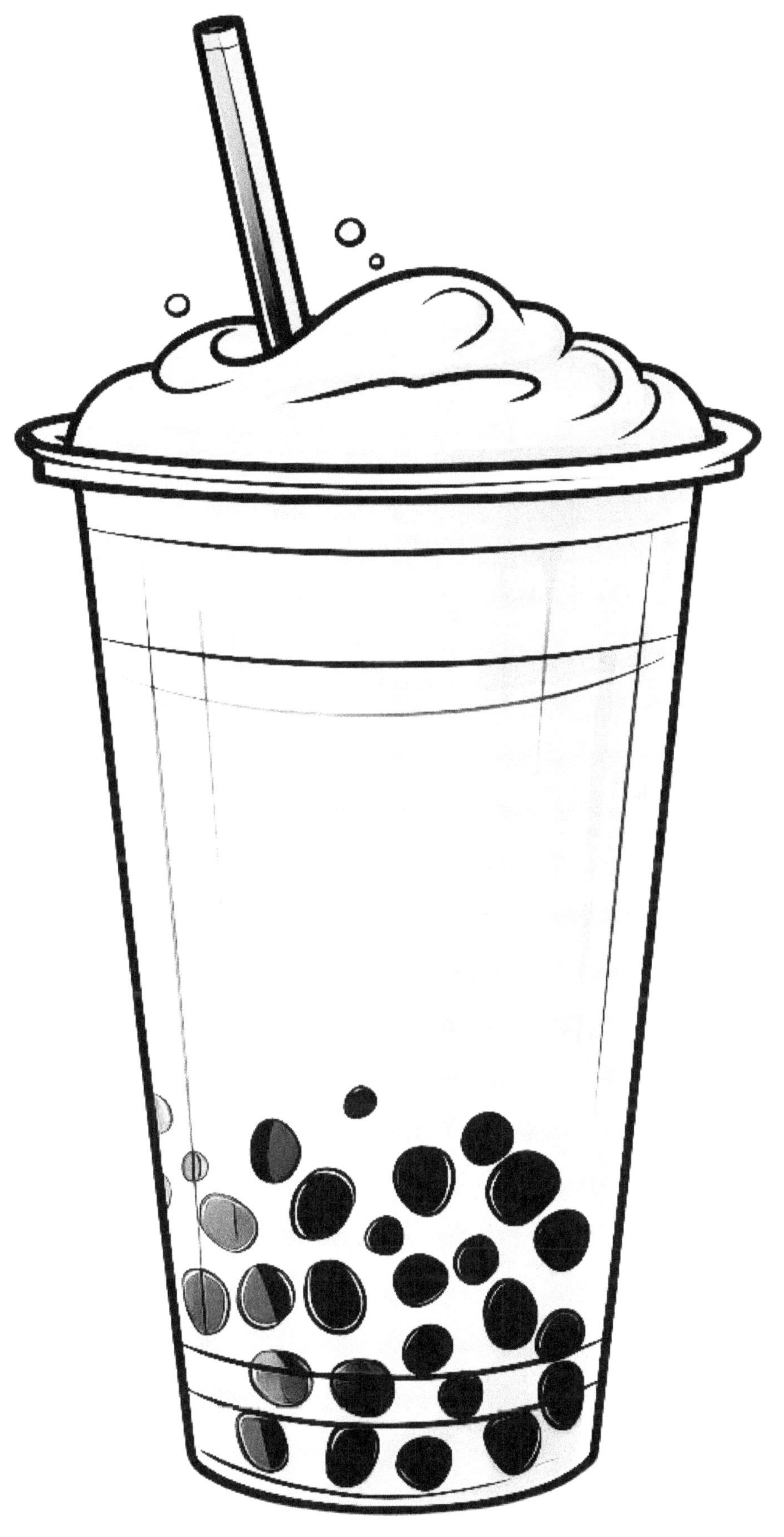

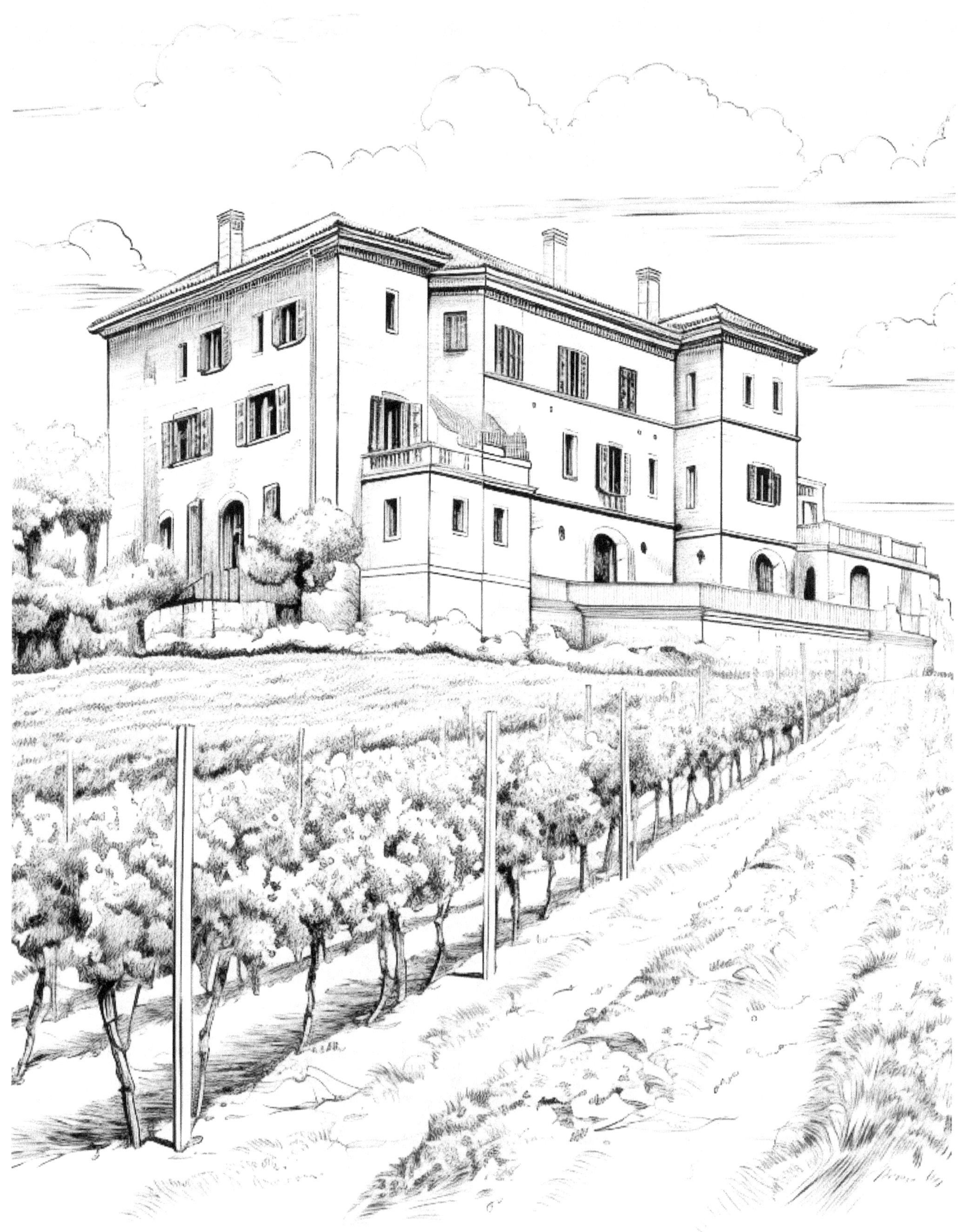

French Chateau

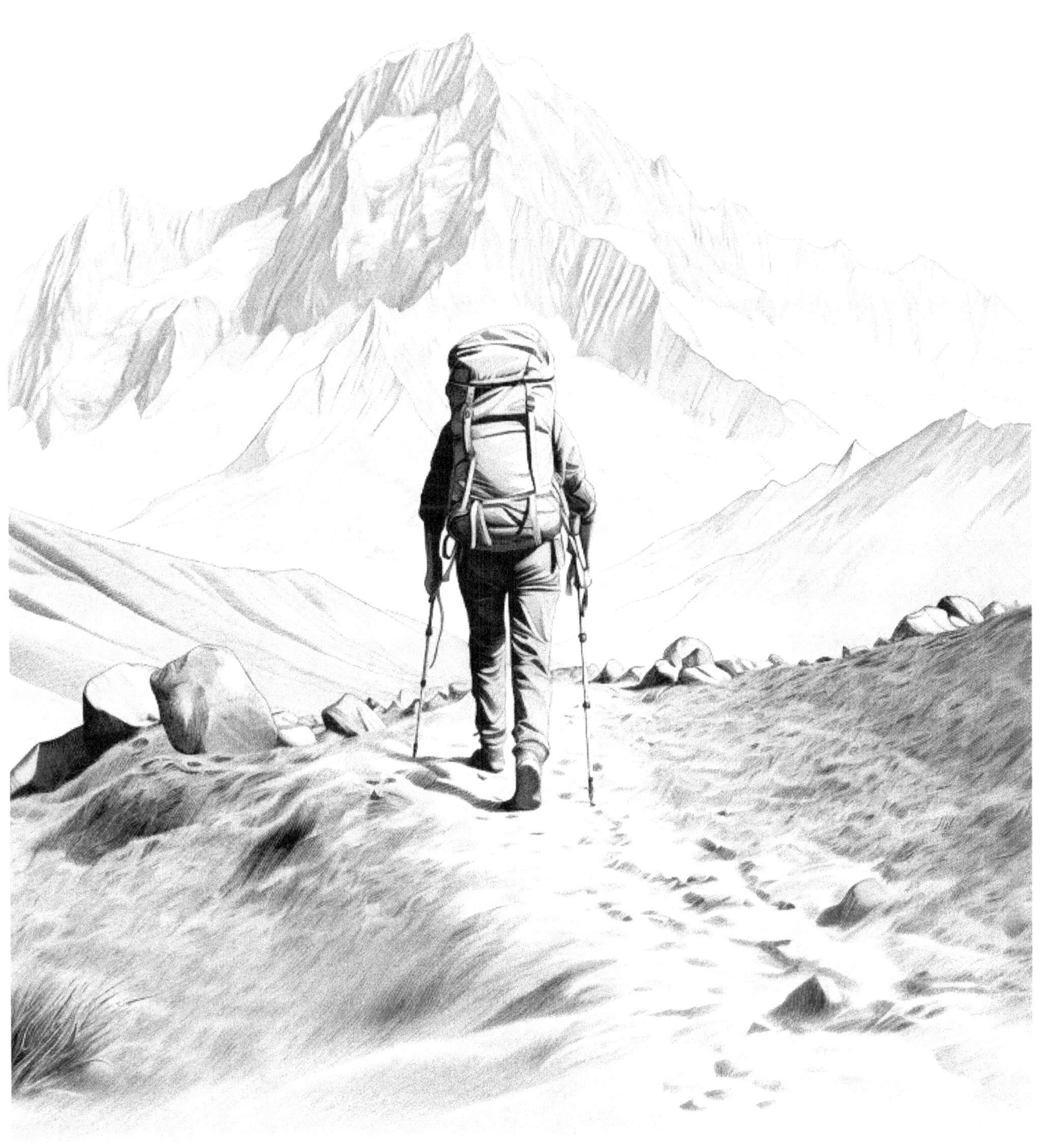

Andes Mountains, Chile

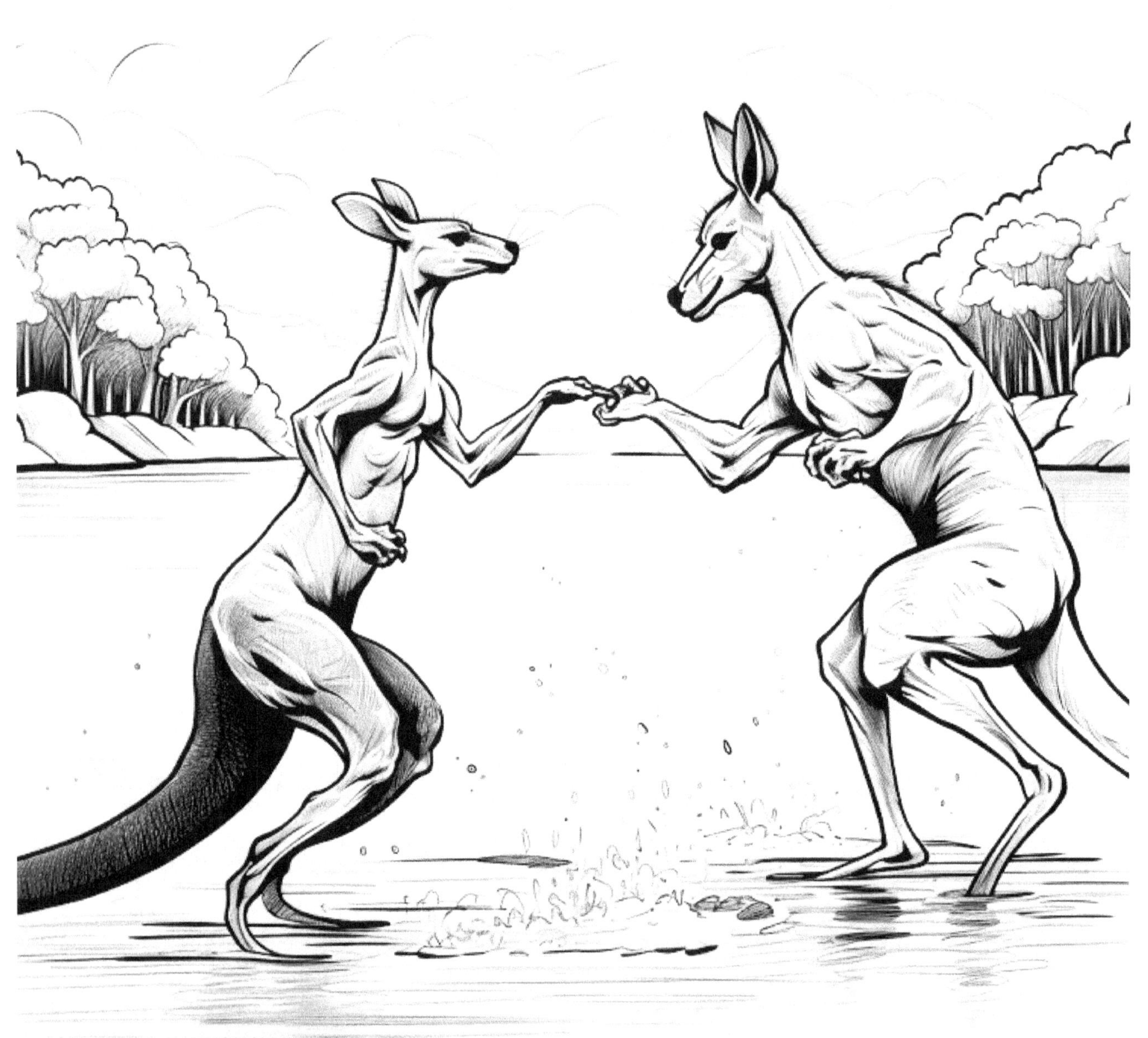

Maldives

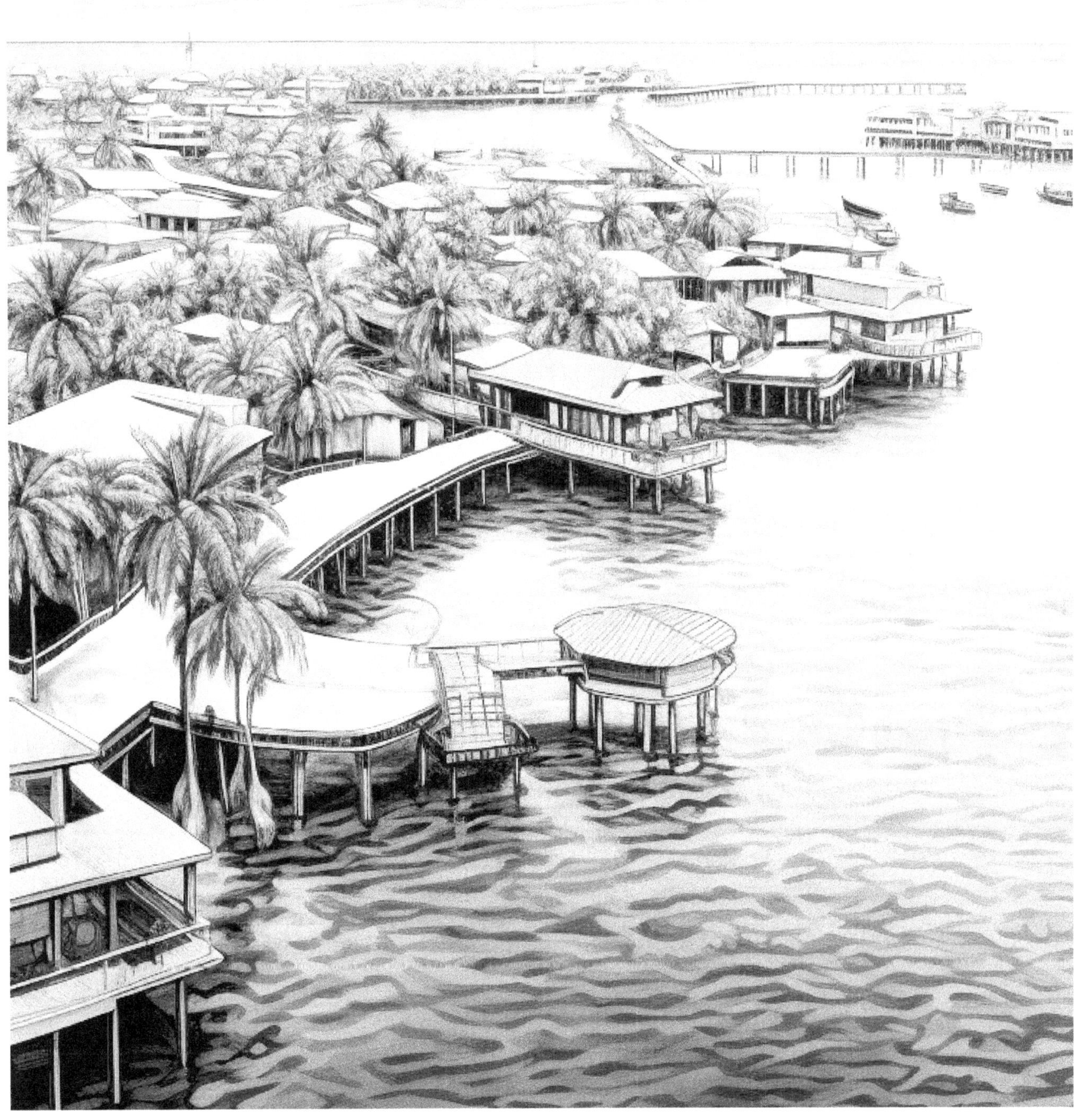

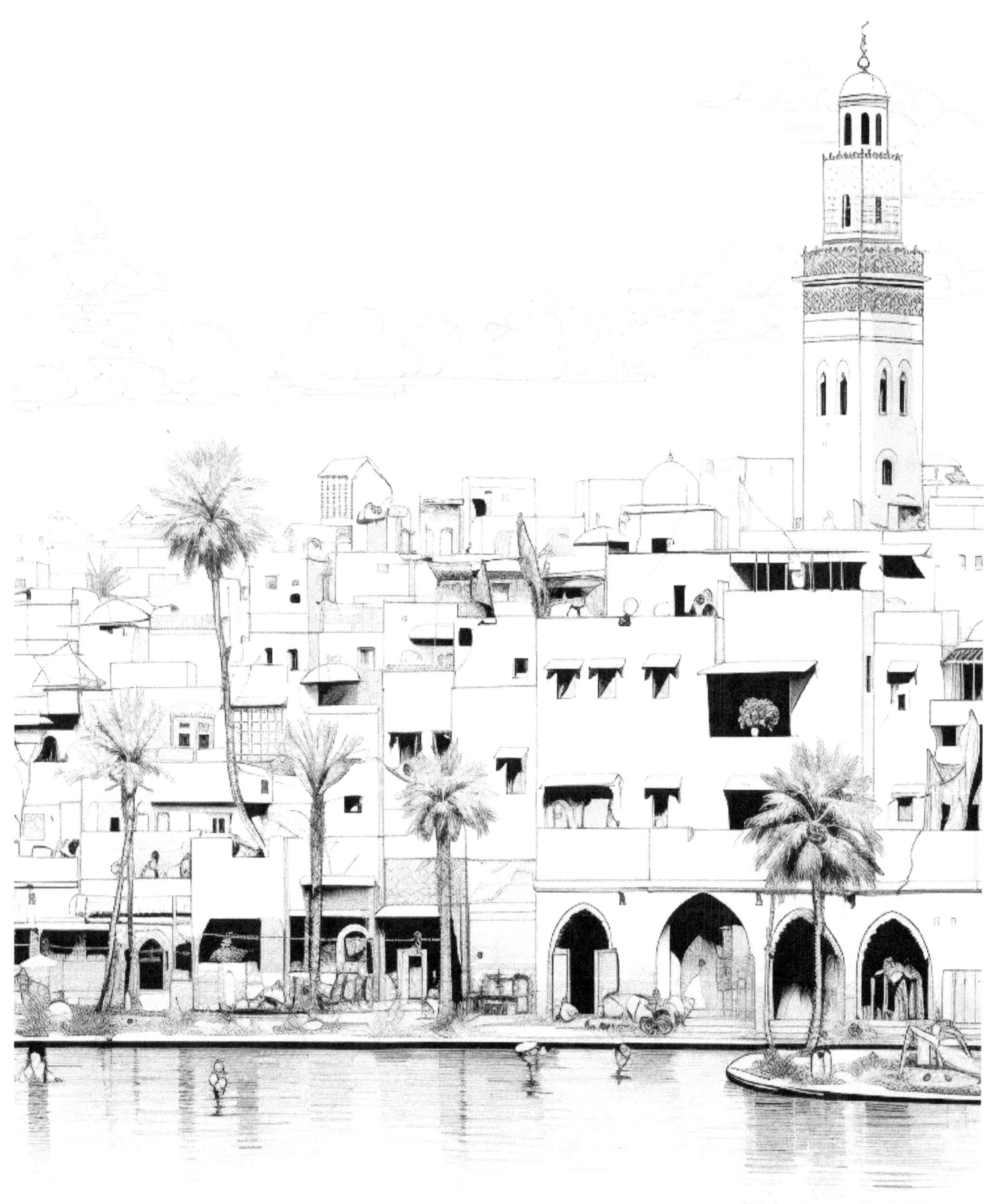

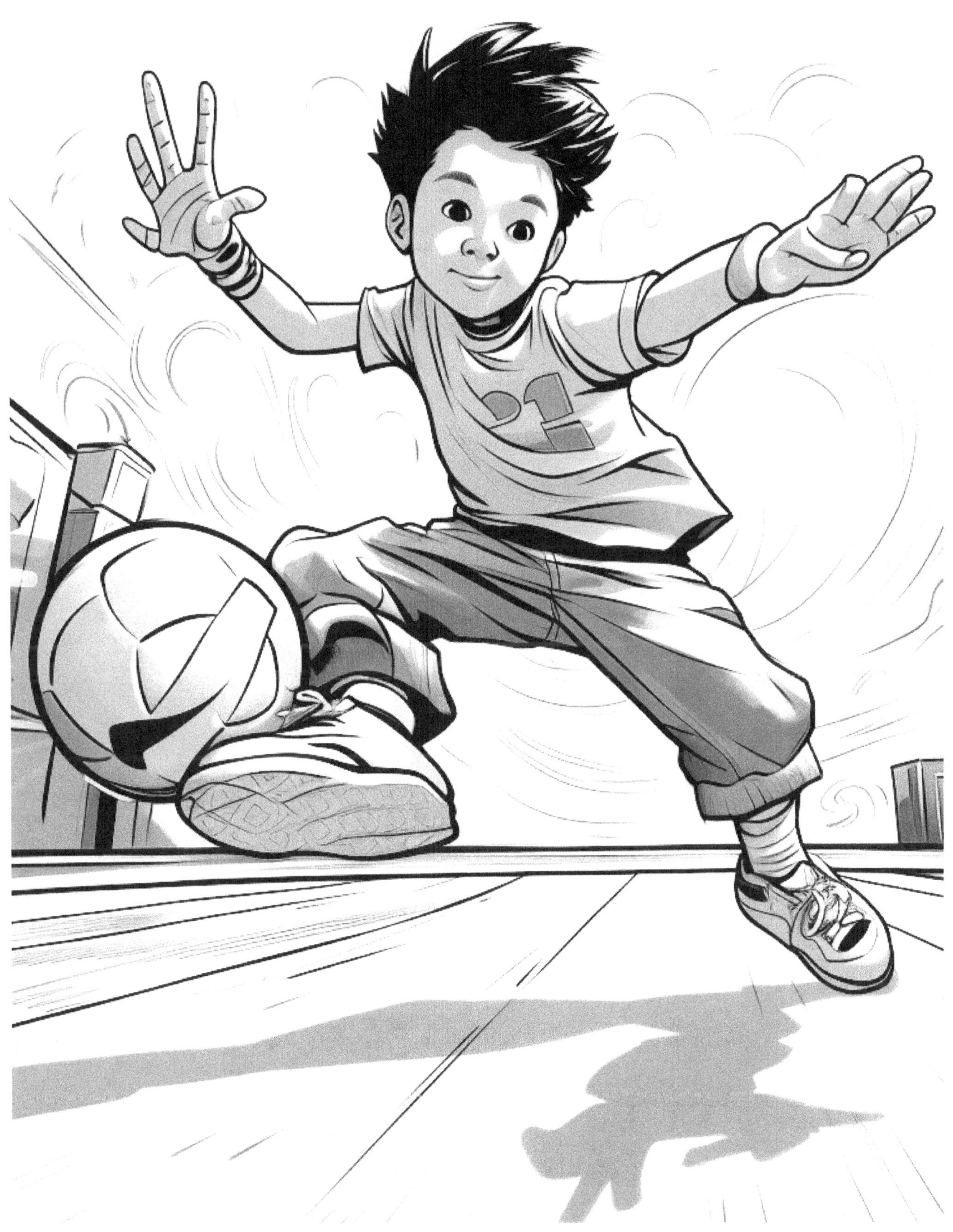

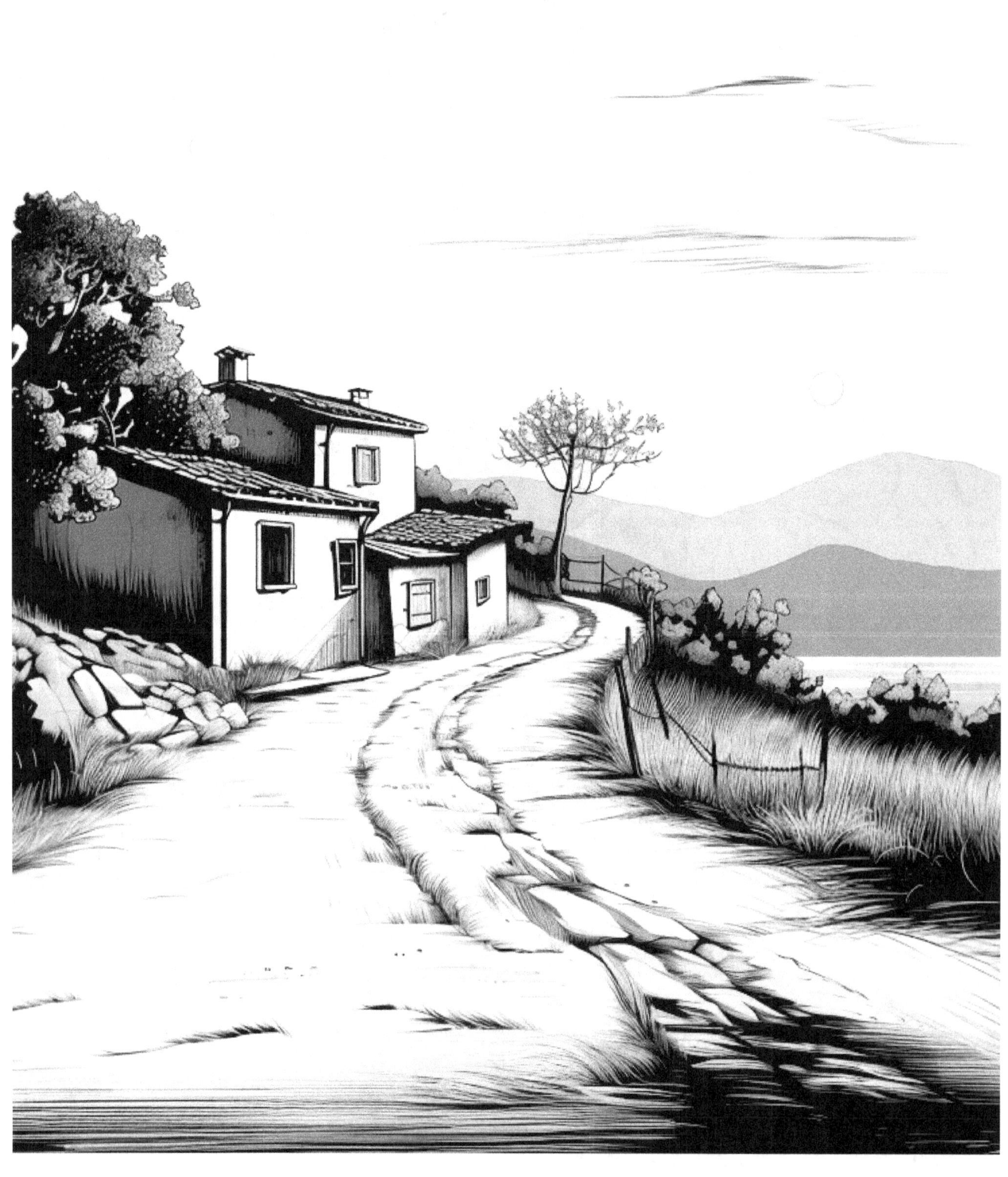

Rural Albania

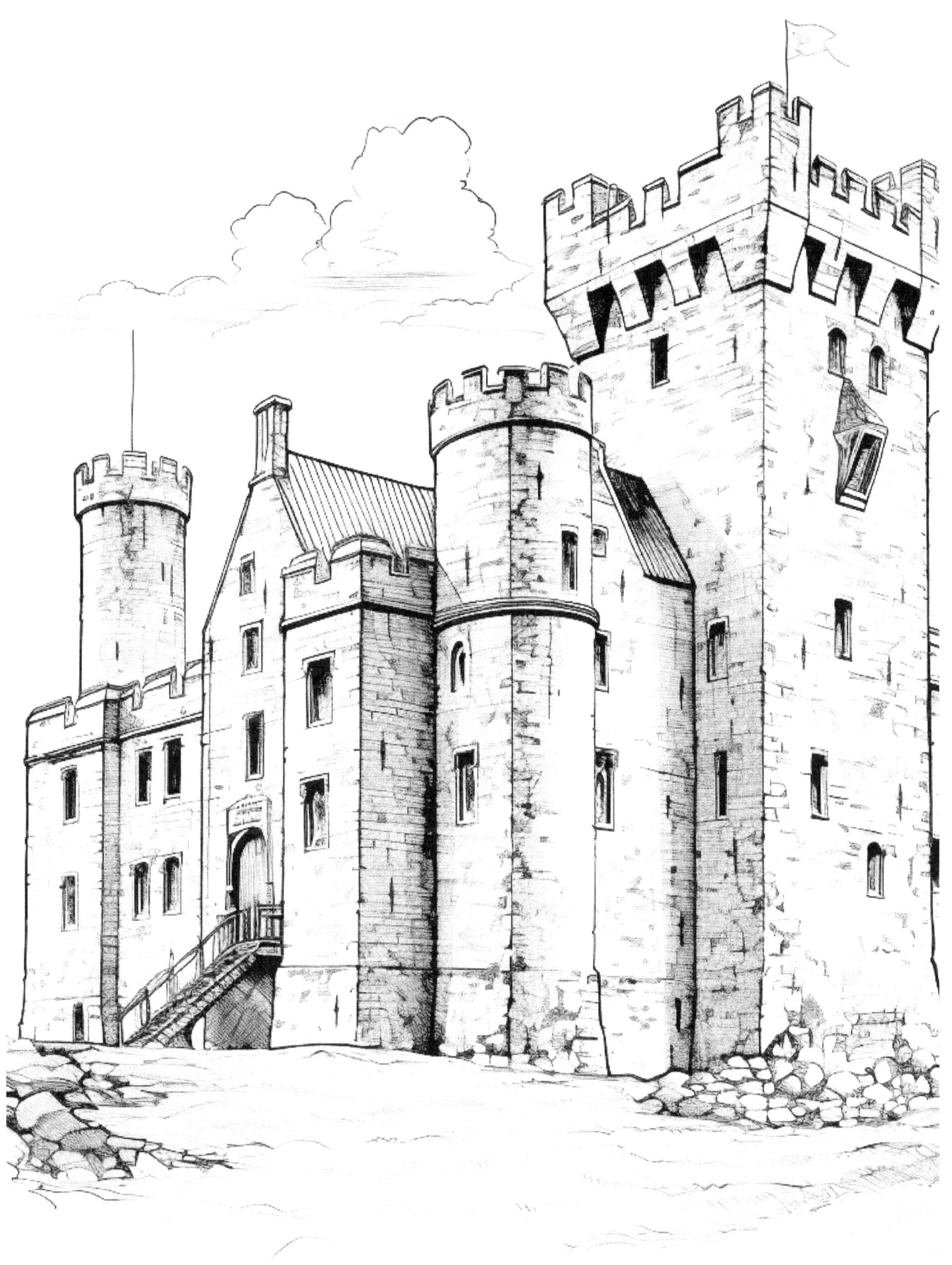

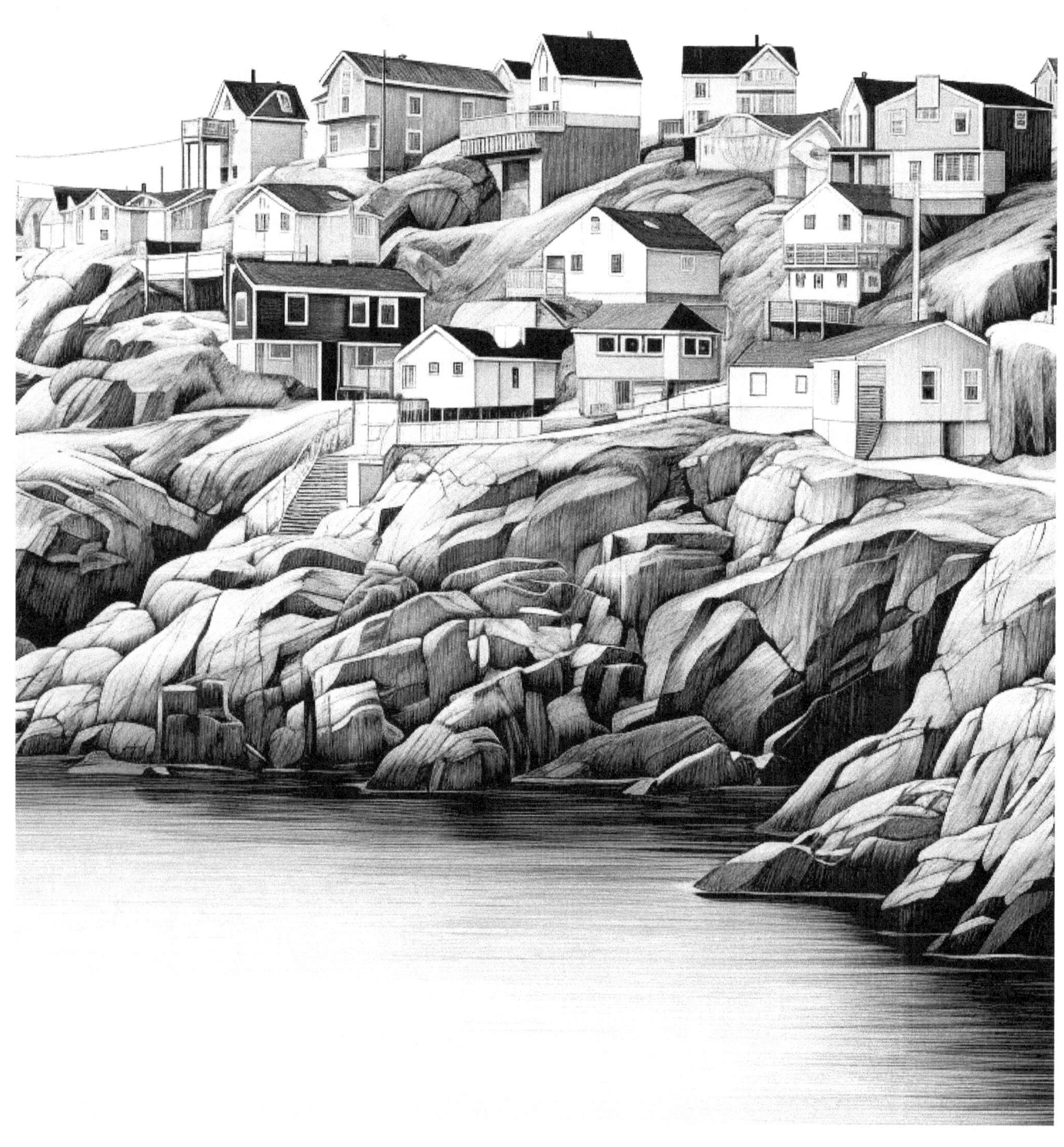

Newfoundland, Canada

Saudi Arabia

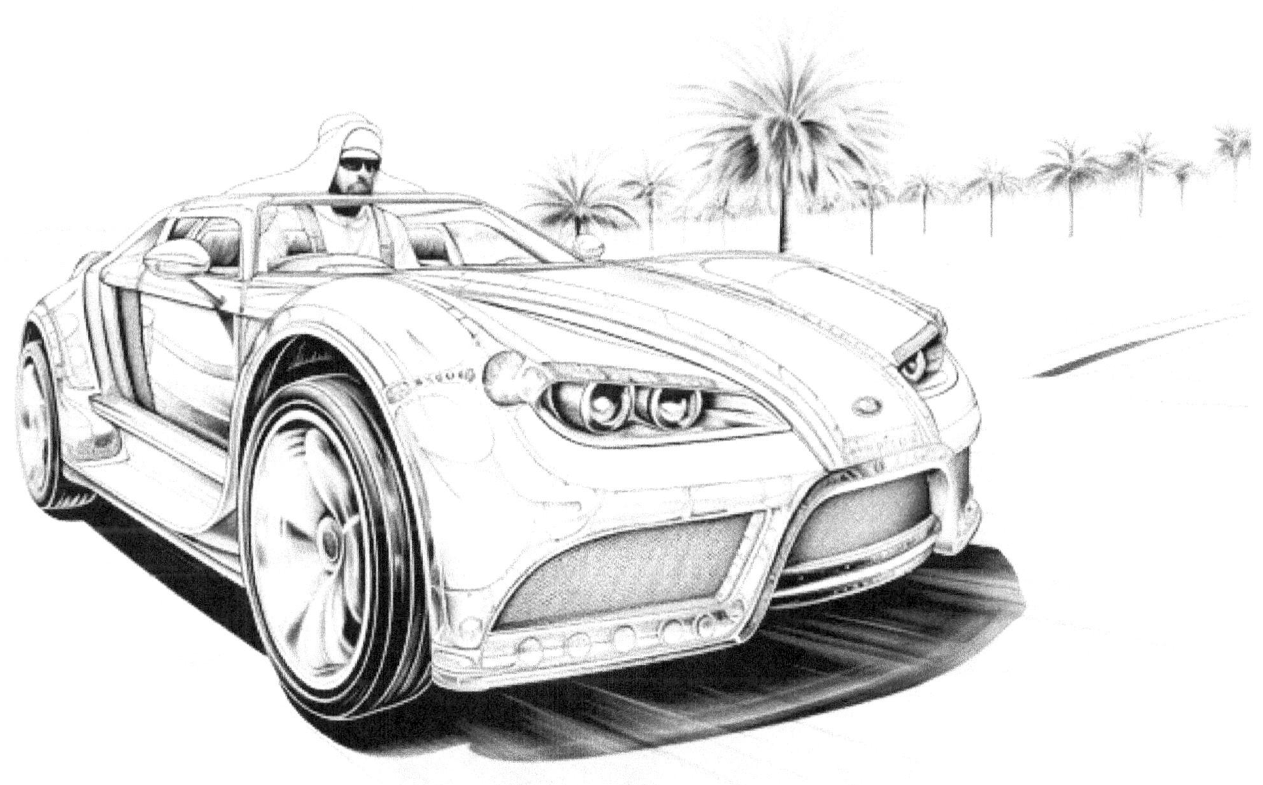

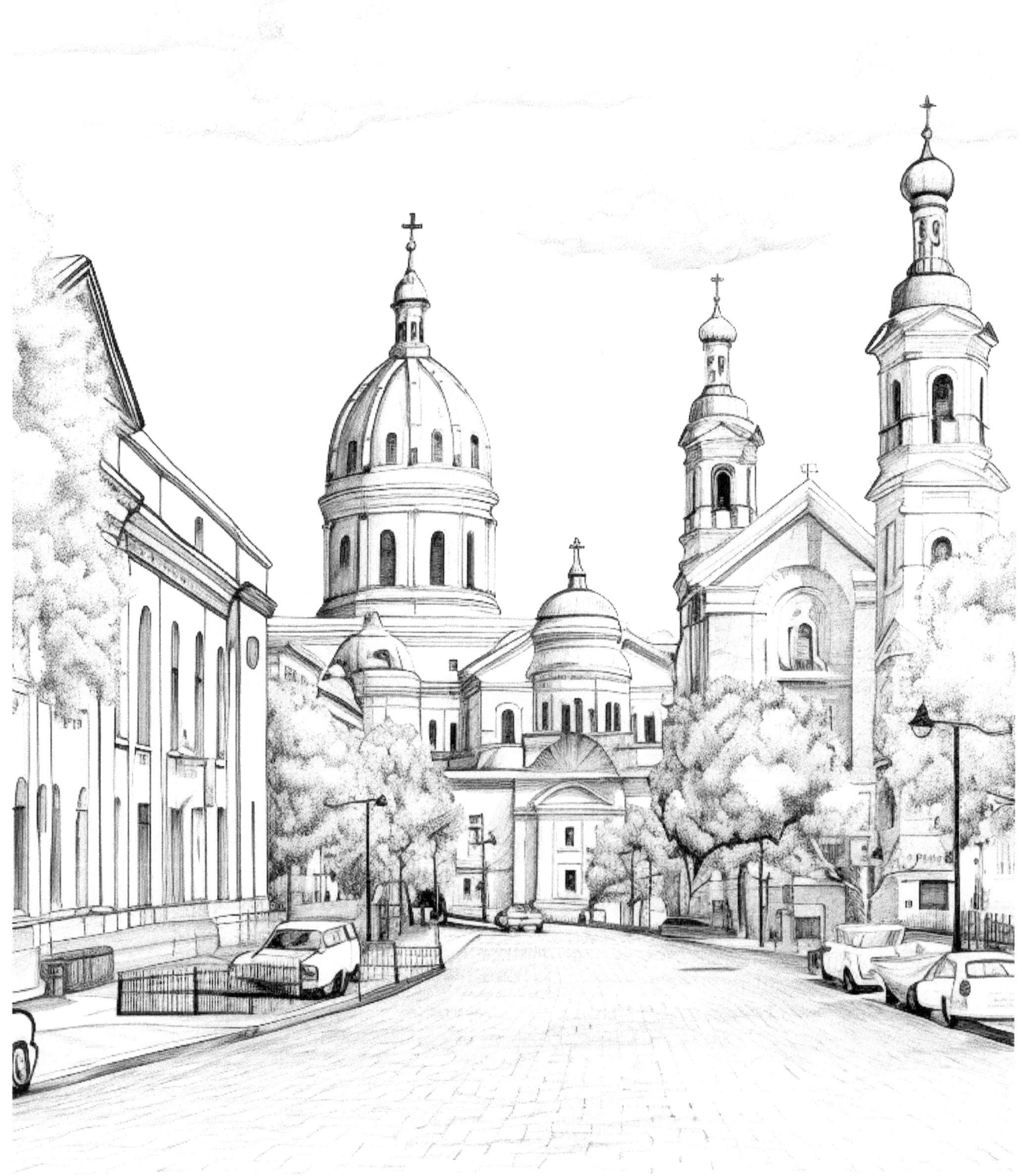

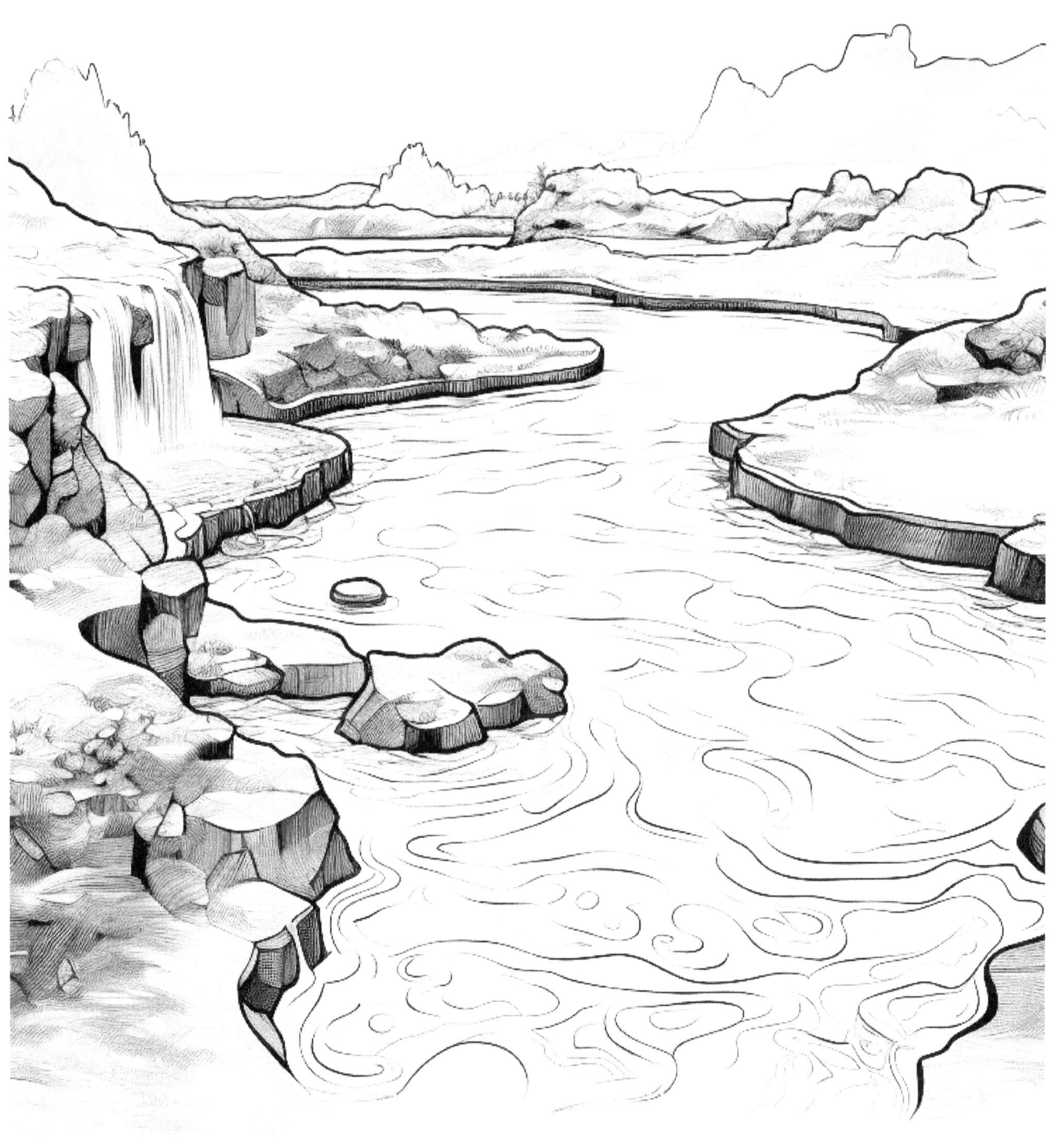

Zanzibar, Tanzania

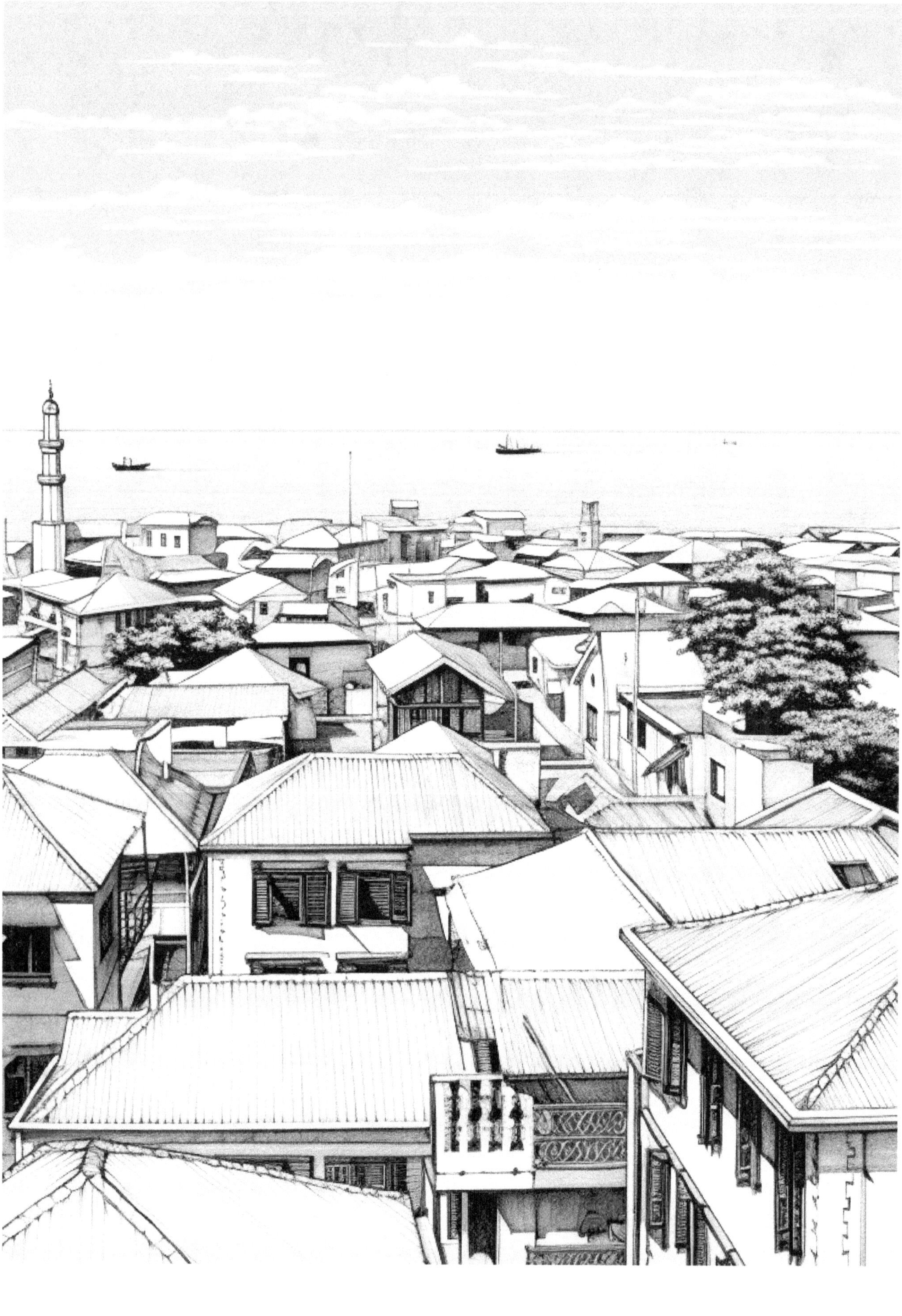

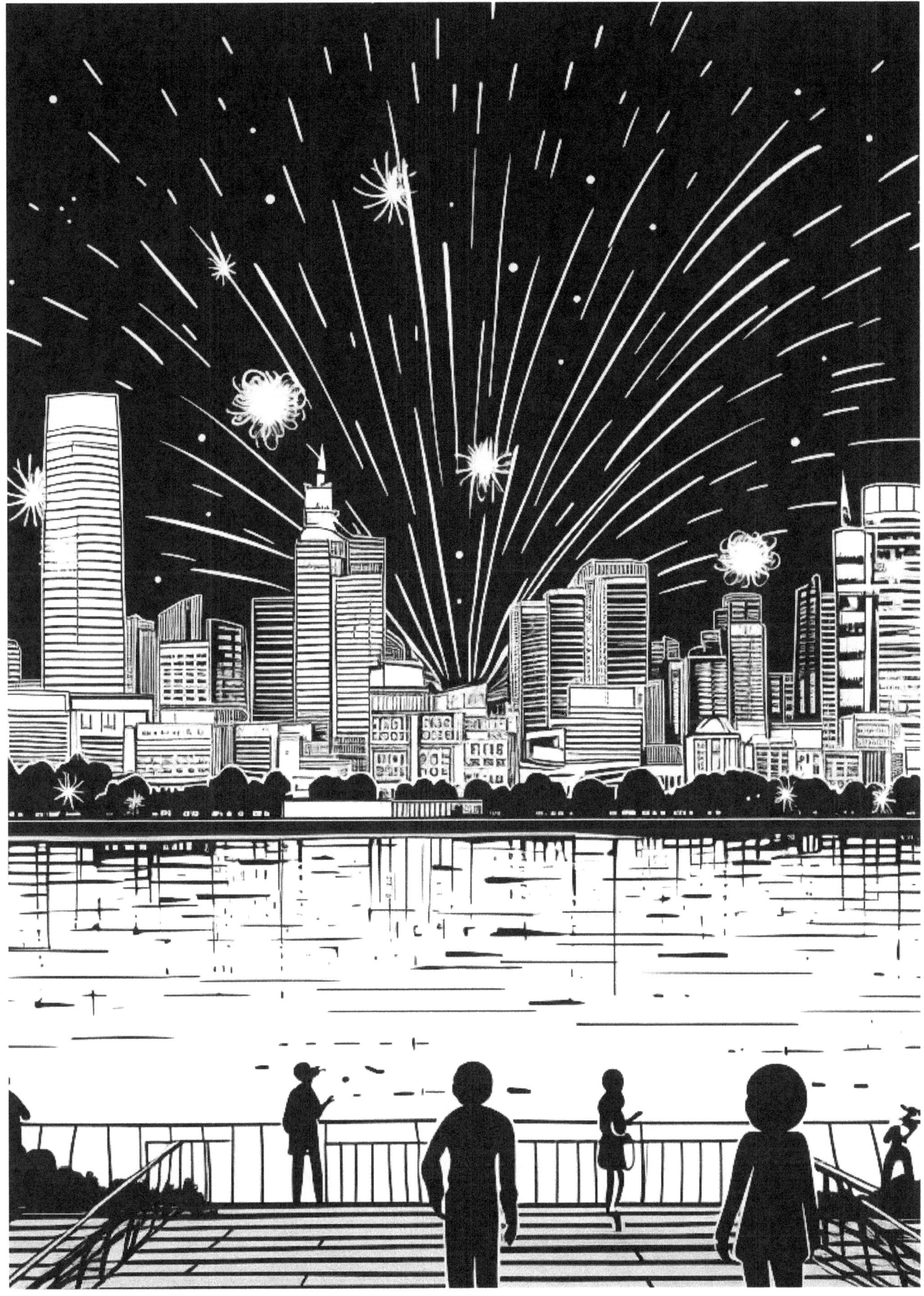

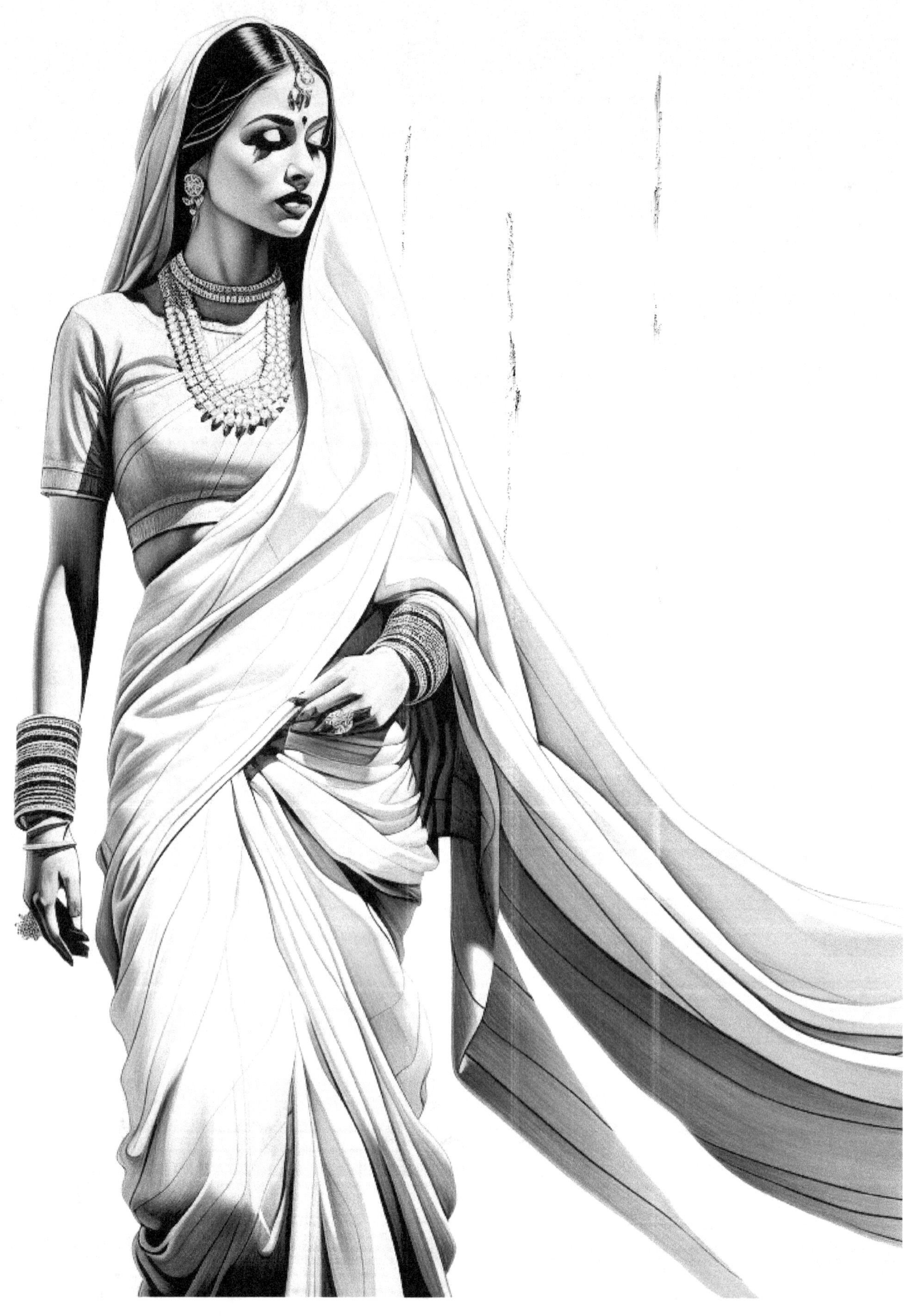

Woman in Saari

Norway

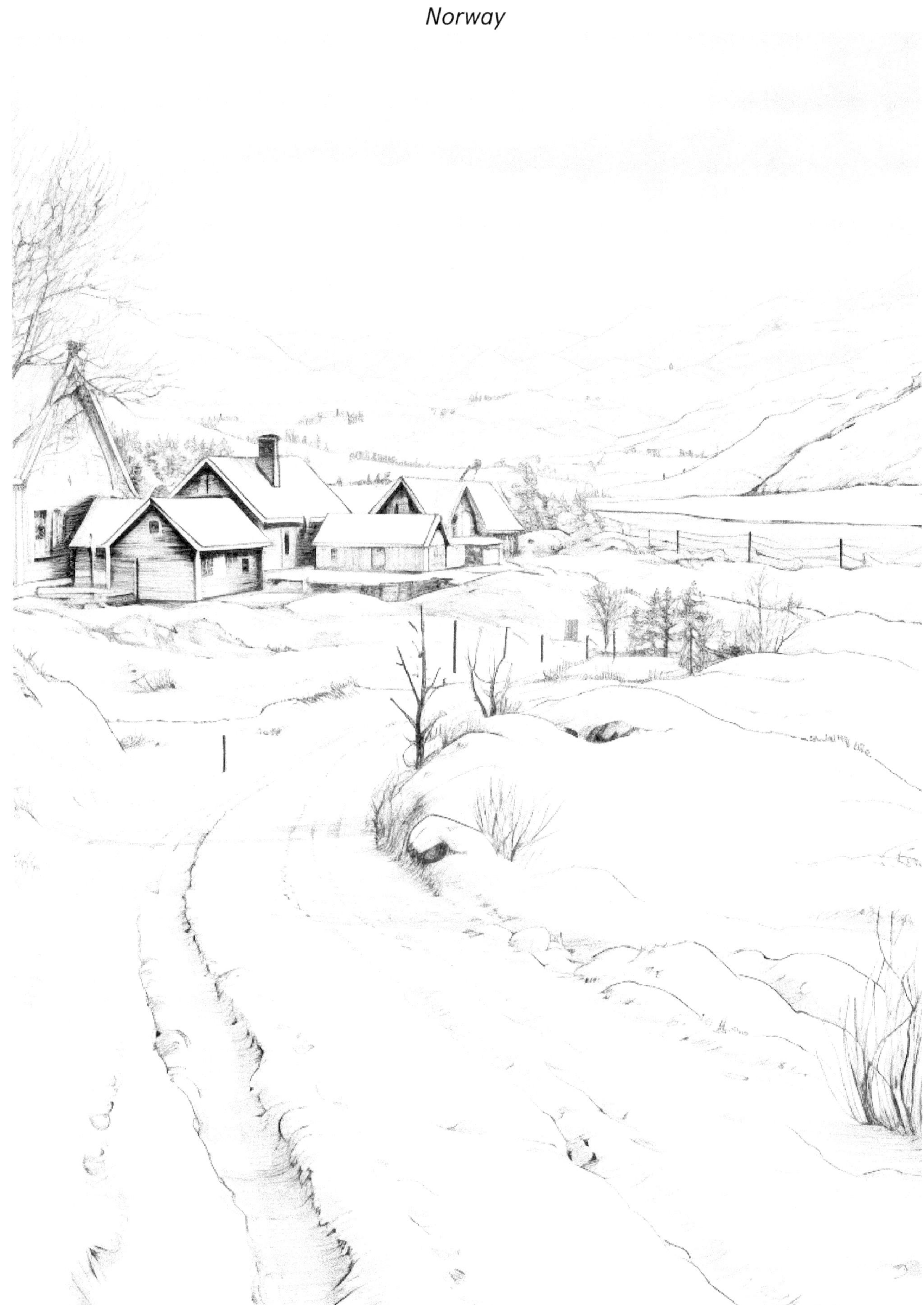

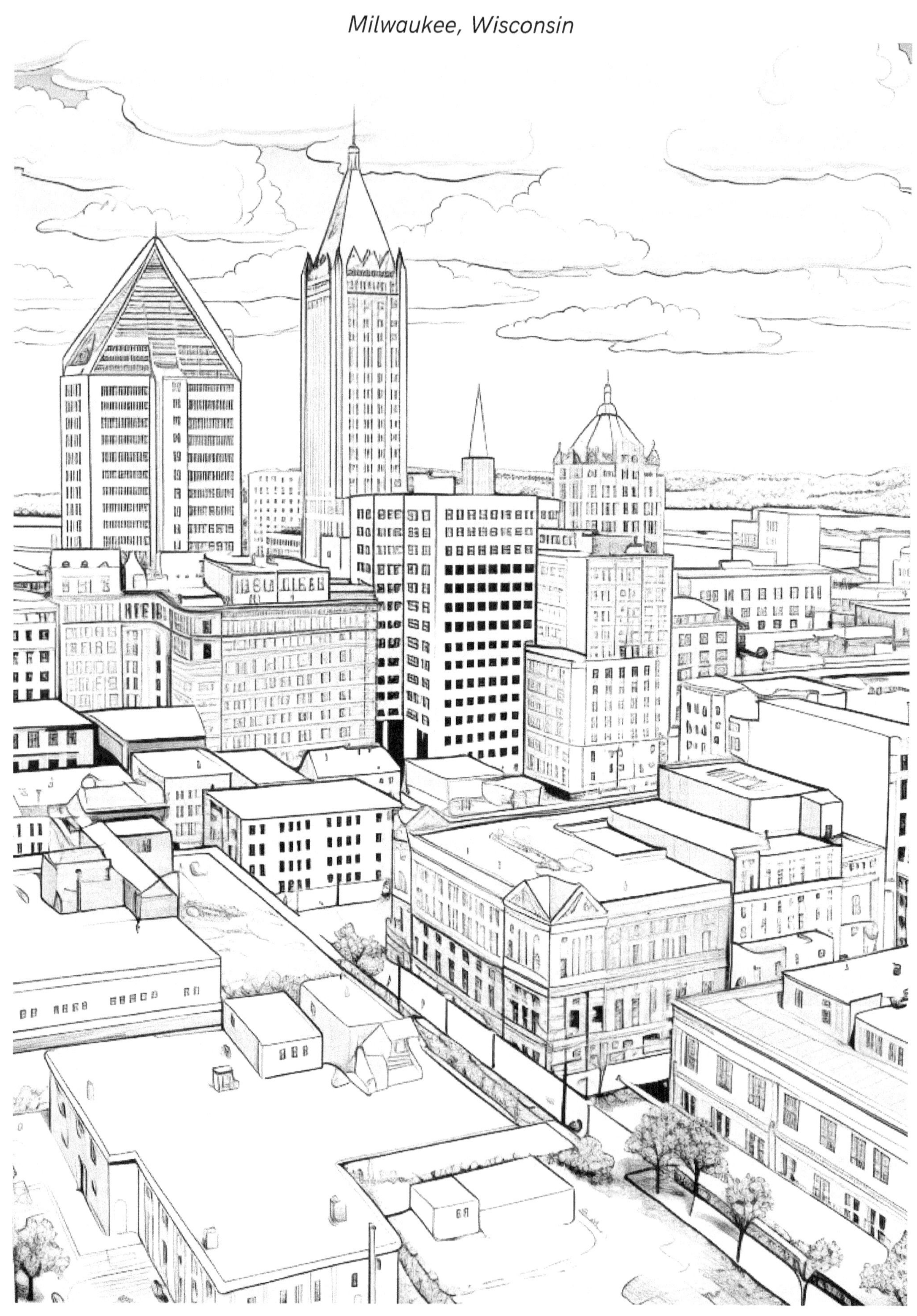

www.ingramcontent.com/pod-product-compliance
Lightning Source LLC
Chambersburg PA
CBHW080226260726
48658CB00008B/3015